New Directions for
Student Services

Elizabeth J. Whitt
EDITOR-IN-CHIEF

John H. Schuh
ASSOCIATE EDITOR

New Directions for Student Services, 1997–2014: Glancing Back, Looking Forward

Elizabeth J. Whitt
John H. Schuh

EDITORS

Number 151 • Fall 2015
Jossey-Bass
San Francisco

NEW DIRECTIONS FOR STUDENT SERVICES, 1997–2014: GLANCING BACK, LOOKING FORWARD
Elizabeth J. Whitt, John H. Schuh (eds.)
New Directions for Student Services, no. 151

Elizabeth J. Whitt, Editor-in-Chief
John H. Schuh, Associate Editor

NEW DIRECTIONS FOR STUDENT SERVICES (ISSN 0164-7970, e-ISSN 1536-0695) is part of The Jossey-Bass Higher and Adult Education Series and is published quarterly by Wiley Subscription Services, Inc., A Wiley Company, at Jossey-Bass, One Montgomery Street, Suite 1200, San Francisco, CA 94104-4594. POSTMASTER: Send address changes to New Directions for Student Services, Jossey-Bass, One Montgomery Street, Suite 1200, San Francisco, CA 94104-4594.

New Directions for Student Services is indexed in CIJE: Current Index to Journals in Education (ERIC), Contents Pages in Education (T&F), Current Abstracts (EBSCO), Education Index /Abstracts (H.W. Wilson), Educational Research Abstracts Online (T&F), ERIC Database (Education Resources Information Center), and Higher Education Abstracts (Claremont Graduate University).

Microfilm copies of issues and articles are available in 16 mm and 35 mm, as well as microfiche in 105 mm, through University Microfilms Inc., 300 North Zeeb Road, Ann Arbor, Michigan 48106-1346.

SUBSCRIPTIONS cost $89 for individuals in the U.S., Canada, and Mexico, and $113 in the rest of the world for print only; $89 in all regions for electronic only; and $98 in the U.S., Canada, and Mexico for combined print and electronic; and $122 for combined print and electronic in the rest of the world. Institutional print only subscriptions are $335 in the U.S., $375 in Canada and Mexico, and $409 in the rest of the world; electronic only subscriptions are $335 in all regions; and combined print and electronic subscriptions are $402 in the U.S., $442 in Canada and Mexico, and $476 in the rest of the world.

EDITORIAL CORRESPONDENCE should be sent to the Editor-in-Chief, Elizabeth J. Whitt, University of California Merced, 5200 North Lake Rd. Merced, CA 95343.

Cover design: Wiley
Cover Images: © Lava 4 images | Shutterstock

www.josseybass.com

CONTENTS

EDITORS' NOTES

When we began our work as editors of *New Directions for Student Services* (*NDSS*) in 1996, we did not imagine that we would be at the helm of this sourcebook series for nearly 20 years. Much to our surprise, though, in spring 2016, almost exactly 2 decades after our first conversation about "Now what?," the final volume for which we have responsibility will be published. Our first issue was #78 (in 1997) and our last will be #153, 77 sourcebooks in all and half the entire *NDSS* series through issue #153.

In 2013, when we notified Jossey-Bass/Wiley that we would retire from the series as of November 1, 2015—the final deadline for delivering issue #153—we did what many "retirees" do: Look back and take stock (along the lines of "What have we accomplished?") and look ahead to the future. This sourcebook—our 75th—is the result of that contemplation, though we have shared the task with a number of good colleagues.

Our collective purpose is to describe and discuss trends over the past 2 decades that have had a significant impact on student affairs practice. This review is not exhaustive nor is it inclusive. There are any number of issues we could have chosen to address but did not. These include organizational changes, changes in professional associations, and "big picture" changes in the landscape of American higher education. We chose, instead, to address six broad topics that encompass the bulk of the foci of the *NDSS* series from 1997 through 2014: (a) student affairs practice, (b) students, (c) assessment, (d) digital technologies, (e) finance, and (f) staff preparation and development.

We begin, in Chapter 1, with a review of the topics covered in the *NDSS* series from 1997 through 2014 and a profile of the guest editors whose work comprised the volumes published during that time. The topical chapters begin with Chapter 2, in which Florence A. Hamrick and Krista Klein describe changes that have influenced student affairs practice.

In Chapter 3, Jillian Kinzie describes changes in undergraduate students over the past 2 decades by tracing the evolution of student characteristics and student affairs responses to those changes. She also provides a look into the future, based on her review of the past.

Assessment in student affairs is the focus of Becki Elkins in Chapter 4. This chapter provides an overview of the history of assessment in student affairs in recent decades, considers current practice, and offers recommendations for the future.

The challenges and potentials of student affairs practice in the digital age are addressed by Edmund T. Cabellon and Reynol Junco in Chapter 5. Some of the topics they consider include expanding technologies, social media, and the impact of digital revolutions on working effectively with students.

New Directions for Student Services, no. 151, Fall 2015 © 2015 Wiley Periodicals, Inc.
Published online in Wiley Online Library (wileyonlinelibrary.com) • DOI: 10.1002/ss.20132

Chapter 6 examines contemporary issues in student affairs budgeting and finance. Ann M. Gansemer-Topf and Peter D. Englin look at recent history of these topics and offer suggestions for dealing with the financial challenges of the future.

In Chapter 7, Anna M. Ortiz, Ilinca Filimon, and Monica Cole-Jackson review changes in the preparation of student affairs educators over the past 2 decades and discuss issues related to development of student affairs professionals.

The volume concludes with Chapter 8, in which we offer some thoughts about student affairs practice in the foreseeable future, based in part on what we and our colleagues have learned from looking at the recent past.

As a final note, we are grateful for the good work of our colleagues on this volume, and for the time, effort, patience, and collaboration of all the guest editors with whom we have worked in the past 18 years. Their contributions to the literature of student affairs have been what we intended when we began this journey: interesting, provocative, useful, and timely.

Elizabeth J. Whitt
John H. Schuh
Editors

ELIZABETH J. WHITT is vice provost and dean for undergraduate education and professor of sociology at University of California, Merced.

JOHN H. SCHUH is director of the Emerging Leaders Academy and distinguished professor emeritus at Iowa State University.

1

This chapter describes and discusses the topics covered in the New
Directions for Student Services *sourcebook series from 1997
through 2014 and provides a profile of the guest editors for the
series.*

Glancing Back at *New Directions for Student Services*, 1997–2014

Elizabeth J. Whitt, John H. Schuh

When we began our work as editors of *New Directions for Student Services* (*NDSS*) in 1996, we did not imagine that we would be at the helm of this sourcebook series for nearly 20 years. Much to our surprise, though, in spring 2016, almost exactly 2 decades after our first conversation about "Now what?," the final volume for which we have responsibility will be published. Our first issue was #78 (in 1997), and our last will be #153: 77 sourcebooks in all and half the entire *NDSS* series through issue #153.

In 2013, when we notified Jossey-Bass/Wiley that we would retire from the series as of November 1, 2015, the final deadline for delivering issue #153, we decided it was a good time to look at those 72 sourcebooks as a whole, something we had not done often in the midst of making sure we produced four high-quality issues a year. This sourcebook—our 75th—is the result of that look backward at 1997 through 2014. We focused on three questions for our retrospective: First, who have served as our guest editors, the people without whom the series would not exist? Second, what topics have we addressed over the years? And, third, in what, if any, ways are the volumes published from 1997 through 2014 different from or similar to the 77 volumes that preceded them? In this chapter, we provide a brief description of our answers to those questions. Table 1.1 identifies the *NDSS* sourcebooks from 1997 through 2014.

We begin, however, with a brief framework of what *NDSS* purports to be. On the publisher's website (Wiley Online Library, 2014) *NDSS* is characterized this way:

> This quarterly monograph is filled with the latest research on student services in the higher education field. Each volume in the series is a completely self-contained, fully indexed edited collection featuring contributions from some of the top minds in the field. (para. 1)

New Directions for Student Services, no. 151, Fall 2015 © 2015 Wiley Periodicals, Inc.
Published online in Wiley Online Library (wileyonlinelibrary.com) • DOI: 10.1002/ss.20133

Table 1.1. NDSS Titles: 1997–2014

Issue Number/Year	Title	First Editor
78—1997	Using Technology to Promote Student Learning	Engstrom
79—1997	Serving Students at Metropolitan Universities	Dietz
80—1997	Helping African American Men Succeed	Cuyjet
81—1998	New Challenges for Greek Letter Organizations	Whipple
82—1998	Beyond Law and Policy	Cooper
83—1998	Responding to the New Affirmative Action Climate	Gehring
84—1998	Strategies for Staff Development	Bryan
85—1999	Student Affairs Research, Evaluation, and Assessment	Malaney
86—1999	Beyond Borders	Dalton
87—1999	Creating Successful Partnerships: Academic and Student Affairs	Schuh
88—1999	Understanding and Applying Cognitive Development Theory	Love
89—2000	The Role Student Aid Plays in Enrollment Management	Coomes
90—2000	Powerful Programming for Student Learning	Liddell
91—2000	Serving Students with Disabilities	Belch
92—2000	Leadership and Management Issues for a New Century	Woodard
93—2001	Student Services for Athletes	Howard-Hamilton
94—2001	Consumers, Adversaries, and Partners: Families	Daniel
95—2001	The Implications of Student Spirituality for Student Affairs	Jablonski
96—2001	Developing External Partnerships for Enhanced Service	Dietz
97—2002	Working with Asian American College Students	McEwan
98—2002	Art and Practical Wisdom of Student Affairs Leadership	Dalton
99—2002	Addressing Contemporary Campus Safety Issues	Wilkinson
100—2002	Student Affairs and External Relations	Snyder
101—2002	Planning and Achieving Successful Student Affairs Facilities Projects	Price
102—2003	Meeting the Special Needs of Adult Students	Kilgore
103—2003	Contemporary Financial Issues	Schuh
104—2003	Meeting the Needs of African American Women	Howard-Hamilton
105—2004	Addressing the Needs of Latino American Students	Ortiz
106—2004	Serving the Millennial Generation	Coomes
107—2004	Programs and Services for Men	Kellom
108—2004	Using Entertainment Media in Teaching and Practice	Forney
109—2005	Serving Native American Students	Fox
110—2005	Developing Social Justice Allies	Reason
111—2005	Gender Identity and Sexual Orientation	Sanlo
112—2005	Technology and Student Affairs	Kruger
113—2006	Gambling on Campus	McClellan
114—2006	Understanding Students in Transition	Laanan
115—2006	Supporting Graduate and Professional Students	Guentzel
116—2006	The Small College Dean	Westfall
117—2007	Student Affairs Staff as Teachers	Moore
118—2007	Key Issues in Enrollment Management	Crady
119—2007	e-Portfolios	Garis

Table 1.1. (Continued)

Issue Number/Year	Title	First Editor
120—2007	Responding to the Realities of Race on Campus	Harper
121—2008	Assisting Bereaved College Students	Servaty-Seib
122—2008	Managing Parent Partnerships	Carney-Hall
123—2008	Biracial and Multiracial Students	Renn
124—2008	Using Emerging Technologies to Enhance Student Engagement	Junco
125—2008	NASPA Supplement—Campus Violence	Jablonski
125—2009	Intersections of Religious Privilege	Watt
126—2009	Creating a Veteran-Friendly Campus	Ackerman
127—2009	Case Studies for Implementing Assessment in Student Affairs	Bresciani
128—2009	Dealing with the Behavior and Psychological Problems of Students	Dunkle
129—2010	Student Affairs Budgeting and Financial Management	Varlotta
130—2010	Advancement Work in Student Affairs	Miller
131—2010	Understanding and Supporting Undocumented Students	Price
132—2010	Strategic Planning in Student Affairs	Ellis
133—2011	Emerging Issues and Practices in Peer Education	Williams
134—2011	Fostering the Increased Integration of Students with Disabilities	Huger
135—2011	Advancing the Integrity of Professional Practice	Young
136—2011	Supporting and Supervising Midlevel Professionals	Roper
137—2012	Enhancing Sustainability Campus Wide	Jacobs
138—2012	Stepping Up to Stepping Out: Life After College	McClellan
139—2012	Facilitating the Moral Growth of Students	Liddell
140—2012	Developing Students' Leadership Capacity	Guthrie
141—2013	Preventing College Student Suicide	Taub
142—2013	Selected Contemporary Assessment Issues	Schuh
143—2013	Positive Psychology and Appreciative Inquiry	Mather
144—2013	Creating Successful Multicultural Initiatives	Watt
145—2014	The State of the College Union	Yakaboski
146—2014	Undergraduate Global Experiences	Highum
147—2014	Research-Driven Practice in Student Affairs	Martin
148—2014	Strategic Directions for Career Services	Smith

Further, the aims and scope of *NDSS* are as follows:

> Launched in 1978, *New Directions for Student Services* combines knowledge from current research and theories with the best thinking about practice to address issues of concern and interest to those who work with—or have responsibility for policies and programs regarding—college students. (para. 2)

According to the website, key words associated with *NDSS* include student services, higher education, college administration, and university administration (Wiley Online Library, 2014).

NEW DIRECTIONS FOR STUDENT SERVICES • DOI: 10.1002/ss

Table 1.2. Gender of the Guest Editors

Sex	Number	Percentage
Female	34	47.14
Male	36	52.86

Note: Percentages are rounded to two decimal points.

We think this information is noteworthy because the focus of NDSS has shifted, in part, from concentrating on student services administration to identifying the needs of students and developing strategies to encourage student learning and growth.

Guest Editors

As a bit of background information, each NDSS volume is conceptualized and brought to publication by a guest editor, also referred to as an issue editor. In many cases, a guest editor submitted a proposal to us and after it was accepted, she or he invited authors to contribute chapters to the volume. New Directions is not a refereed journal. It is an editorially reviewed publication that we think exhibits both conceptual as well as editorial rigor, but the manuscripts are not evaluated through a blind review process; the editors of each volume and the editorial team know who the contributors are when they submit their manuscripts.

Women and Men as Guest Editors.   In our analysis of the guest editors of the 72 volumes (#78–#148) under consideration in this chapter, we started by identifying selected characteristics of the editors. Table 1.2 provides a presentation of data related to the gender of the guest editors of NDSS volumes #78 through #148.

In this analysis of the characteristics of the guest editors, for those volumes where more than one person served as guest editor of a volume, we chose the first person listed. That is, if Smith and Jones were listed as the guest editors of a specific volume, we included Smith but not Jones in our sample of editors, which yielded 70 individuals. Had we included volumes with multiple guest editors, the weight of the volumes with just one guest editor would have been diluted. As this table indicates, the editors were nearly evenly divided: 34 (47.14%) women and 36 (52.86%) men. By the way, we did not intentionally select a woman or a man to serve as guest editor of any volume.

Those who served as guest editors typically were well-experienced writers and editors. Whether the gender of our guest editors reflects the field or not is unknown to us, but our guess is that women are slightly underrepresented as guest editors when compared with the field and professoriate over the years. For example, women outnumbered men in the category of executive/administrative/managerial staff in fall 2011 (Snyder & Dillow, 2013, Table 286).

Table 1.3. Gender of Guest Editor by Quintile

Volume Number	Years	Female	Percentage	Male	Percentage
78–91	1997–2000	4	28.6	10	71.4
92–105	2000–2004	9	64.3	5	35.7
106–119	2004–2007	6	42.9	8	57.1
120–133	2007–2011	7	50.0	7	50.0
134–147	2011–2014	8	57.1	6	42.9

Note: Percentages are rounded to two decimal points.

We also attempted to determine whether more women or men served as guest editors over time. Hence, we divided the volumes into quintiles and then determined if a pattern emerged as to when women and men served as guest editors. Table 1.3 summarizes these data.

These data suggest that there was no pattern after the first two quintiles of publications. In the first quintile more men than women served as issue editors but in the second quintile the opposite was true. Thereafter, the same number of men and women served as guest editors. Although we did not take a person's gender into account when offering invitations to guest editors, it turned out that we appointed exactly the same number of women and men for the last 10 years that we have served as the editorial team.

Guest Editors' Professional Roles. Student affairs educators, according to Komives and Carpenter (2009), fit along a continuum from practitioner-practitioners to scholar-scholars. Therefore, it is common for members of the profession to contribute to its literature. Because *NDSS* consists primarily of work that is designed to use research and scholarship to reflect and advance effective practices in student affairs, we wondered in hindsight if the issue editors had tended to be faculty members, student affairs educators, or perhaps a combination of both. This led to our second analysis, that of the primary professional roles of our guest editors. It is important to note that many student affairs practitioners hold part-time, adjunct, lecturer, clinician, or other faculty roles. Therefore, they may be afforded faculty rank and perhaps status as a graduate faculty member. Our concern for this part of the analysis was to identify the primary role of the guest editors, so those guest editors who held a part-time faculty appointment and were primarily student affairs practitioners on their campus were considered to be administrators for the purposes of this analysis. Data related to the professional roles of the guest editors are presented in Table 1.4.

Table 1.4. Guest Editor by Professional Role

Professional Position	Number	Percentage
Faculty	34	48.57
Administrator	36	51.43

Table 1.5. Guest Editor Professional Role Over Time

Volume Number	Years	Faculty Member	Percentage	Administrator	Percentage
78–91	1997–2000	9	64.3	5	35.7
92–105	2000–2004	7	50.0	7	50.0
106–119	2004–2007	6	42.9	8	57.1
120–133	2007–2011	7	50.0	7	50.0
134–147	2011–2014	5	35.7	9	64.3

As the data in Table 1.4 indicate, about as many faculty as administrators served as guest editors. Over the years the student affairs literature has been written frequently by student affairs administrators as well as full-time faculty. Examples of such student affairs administrators include Art Sandeen, Margaret Barr, Lee Upcraft, and Phyllis Mable. Faculty members also have made significant contributions to the literature including such authors as George Kuh, Nancy Evans, Marcia Baxter Magolda, Ernie Pascarella, Pat King, and Pat Terenzini. Still others have served both as student affairs practitioners and faculty and contributed to the literature in both of their roles, such as Susan Komives and Doug Woodard. In the case of our volumes, the split between faculty and student affairs educators probably reflects student affairs as an applied discipline. Patton and Harper (2009), for example, described some of the tensions between theory and practice in student affairs administration and in the end asserted that theory can be used to inform sensemaking and reflection for student affairs practitioners.

We wondered if there was a relationship between time and professional role of guest editors, so we looked the volumes again on a quintile basis to determine if we could tease out any differences over time. Table 1.5 presents these data.

As the data included in the table indicate, during the first quintile, more faculty members than administrators served as a guest editor, by a ratio of nearly 2:1. For the next three quintiles, the number of faculty and student affairs practitioners who served as guest editors was nearly even, with just one more administrator serving as guest editor than faculty members. For the last quintile, the number of administrators exactly reversed the number of faculty for the first quintile. In the end, no patterns emerged from this analysis other than that, by using service as a guest editor of NDSS as a measure, student affairs as an academic discipline continues to experience robust contributions from faculty and administrators to its literature.

Diversity of Guest Editors. The final characteristic we looked at with respect to those who served as guest editors was race/ethnicity of the guest editors. Student affairs practice, to a great extent, has focused on working with students from groups historically underrepresented in higher education, and as Pope and Mueller (2011) pointed out, multicultural competence is important for practitioners. Therefore, we wanted to determine

Table 1.6. Race/Ethnicity of the Guest Editors

Race	Number	Percentage
Person of color	12	17.14
Caucasian	58	82.86

if the guest editors of the 70 sourcebooks under analysis were a diverse group. Table 1.6 provides data with respect to the race/ethnicity of the guest editors.

The data indicate that 12 of the guest editors were from historically underrepresented groups, or 17.14%. This percentage is roughly equivalent to the percentage of people from one or more races who were full-time instructional faculty in degree-granting postsecondary institutions in 2007 (18.2%), 2009 (19.2%), and 2011 (20.7%) (Institute of Education Sciences, 2014, Table 315.20). As was the case with gender and professional roles, we divided the volumes into quintiles to determine if any trends related to time emerged. These data are summarized in Table 1.7.

Again, no clear-cut patterns emerged from this analysis. Only one person of color served as guest editor during the publication of the first 20% of the volumes, but during the next 20%, four persons of color served as guest editors. For the next three quintiles, two or three persons of color served as guest editors. After studying these data we came to the conclusion that no patterns related to the race of the guest editors were apparent.

Content of NDSS

Another purpose of this inquiry was to conduct a cursory analysis of the topics addressed in the 72 volumes we reviewed for this analysis. A few words about how we decided what topics to include in the series might be useful here. As we noted earlier in this chapter, many of the sourcebooks were proposed by guest editors. In evaluating the proposals we received, as well as in determining what volumes to seek editors for, we reviewed current issues in higher education and considered recent trends in relevant research and scholarship. We also scanned program and workshop topics from the national conventions of leading student affairs professional organizations

Table 1.7. Race/Ethnicity of Guest Editors Over Time

Volume Number	Years	Person of Color	Percentage	Caucasian	Percentage
78–91	1997–2000	1	7.14	13	92.96
92–105	2000–2004	4	28.6	10	71.42
106–119	2004–2007	3	21.42	11	78.57
120–133	2007–2011	2	14.29	12	85.71
134–147	2011–2014	2	14.29	12	85.71

and scholarly associations. Conversations with student affairs leaders, including administrators and faculty, were also helpful in identifying topics for *NDSS* volumes.

Because we worked about 2 years ahead on our publication schedule, we typically did not address topics that were "hot" at a particular moment in time. When appropriate, though, we adjusted the queue to respond to emerging issues, such as the quickly evolving financial crisis in higher education, which we addressed by issue #129 in 2010. Also, the leadership of the National Association of Student Personnel Administrators (NASPA) requested inclusion of a "supplement" issue on campus violence in 2008; that volume was #125.

Analysis of the topics of sourcebooks from 1997 through 2014 led to a taxonomy for identifying the categories of titles of the volume. We concede that identifying the categories for the topics and then determining where the volumes fit is a bit arbitrary. For example, should a volume of specialized programming for returning adult students be categorized as addressing the needs of a historically underserved population of students or is it a volume about program development? In that case, the topic of the volume would have been placed in the "underserved student" category rather than the "program development" category but we know a strong case could be made for either category.

The analysis yielded five categories:

1. *Addressing the needs of students from groups historically underrepresented in higher education* [e.g., African American men (#80), students with disabilities (#91 and #134), Asian American students (#97), adult students (#102), African American women (#104), Latino American students (#105), Native American students (#109), biracial and multiracial students (#123), veterans (#126), undocumented students (#131)].

2. *Addressing the needs of all students* [e.g., theories of cognitive development (#88), spirituality (#95), gender identity and sexual orientation (#111), gambling (#113), bereaved students (#121), psychological problems (#128), life after college (#138), moral development (#139), leadership (#140)]

3. *Program development* [e.g., programming for student learning (#90), programs for men (#107), peer education (#133), sustainability (#137), multicultural initiatives (#144), international programs and experiences (#146), career services (#148)].

4. *Student affairs practice* [e.g., technology (#78, #112, and #124); assessment, evaluation, and research (e.g., #85, #119, #127, #142, and #147); enrollment management (e.g., #89 and #118); planning, budgets, and finance (e.g., #101, #103, #129, and #132); leadership and management (e.g., #92, #98,#116, and #120); partnerships on and off campus (e.g., #87, #96, #100, #122, #130)].

Table 1.8. NDSS Topic Analysis (N = 70)

Topic	Number	Percentage
Addressing the needs of students from groups historically underrepresented in higher education	18	25.71
Addressing the needs of all students	11	15.71
Program development	12	17.14
Topics related to student affairs practice	22	31.43
Topics about professional development of student affairs educators	7	10.00

5. *Professional development in student affairs* [e.g., staff development strategies (#84), social justice allies (#110), staff as teachers (#117), integrity in professional practice (#135), midlevel professionals (#136), appreciative inquiry (#143)].

We provide a presentation of our topic analysis in Table 1.8. These data indicate that the topics of the 72 volumes were focused primarily on addressing needs of students (41%) and effective student affairs practice (31%), although those categories encompass a wide range of issues, trends, research, and practice.

Changes Over Time

Because we were also interested in changes over time, we conducted the same analysis as is reflected in Table 1.8 for the 1997–2014 volumes and the first 70 volumes, which were published from 1978 through 1995. A comparison of the topics addressed during those time periods is provided in Table 1.9.

The first 70 volumes focused more on program development (27% vs. 17%) and student affairs practice (40% vs. 31%) than the recent 70 volumes, which placed more emphasis on students (needs of underrepresented

Table 1.9. NDSS Topics for the First and Last 70 Issues

Topic	First 70 Issues Number	First 70 Issues Percentage	Last 70 Issues Number	Last 70 Issues Percentage
Addressing the needs of historically underrepresented populations of students	12	17.14	18	25.71
Addressing the needs of all students	8	11.43	11	15.71
Topics about program development	19	27.14	12	17.14
Topics related to student affairs practice	28	40.00	22	31.43
Topics about professional development of student affairs educators	3	4.29	7	10.00

students, as well as students in general; 41% vs. 28%) and professional development (10% vs. 4%).

Whether these changes were deliberate or intentional is not clear, even to us as editors. We have attempted to address topics that we thought were of interest and use to student affairs educators and the much broader audience who has access to NDSS via subscribers (e.g., libraries); we assume that also was the case for the general editors of the first 70 issues. We do believe, however, that the difference in emphases can be explained in at least three ways.

We focus first on the greater attention paid between 1997 and 2014 to addressing the needs of students (41% vs. 28% of the volumes) and we attribute this change to significant changes in the number and characteristics of those students. As is discussed elsewhere in this sourcebook, the enrollments of colleges and universities have become far more diverse in the past 2 decades than they were when this series was launched in 1978. During the period 1976–2012, roughly the life of this publication, college student enrollments have nearly doubled. In 1976 over 10 million students were enrolled in higher education, but that number grew to over 20 million in 2012 (Institute of Education Sciences, 2014, Table 306.10). So, in terms of sheer numbers, many more people are enrolled in college. But the composition of student bodies has changed dramatically. In 1976, men comprised the majority of college students. By 1979, more women were enrolled than men (50.9% to 49.1%) and by 2012 women comprised 56.8% of all college students (Institute of Education Sciences, 2014, Table 303.10).

Similarly, institutions have become more diverse by race. In 1976, 84.3% of all students identified themselves as White; students of color comprised 15.7% of college student enrollment. By 2012, the percentage of students of color was 39.7%; Whites were 60.3% of all students enrolled (Institute of Education Sciences, 2014, Table 306.10). In addition, the growth in the percentage of all students who are students of color accelerated rapidly over the time period under consideration. For example, the number of White students enrolled in 1976 was 9.076 million, and the number grew to 10.462 million in 2000 and then 11.981 million in 2012. In contrast, the numbers of students of color enrolled grew from 1.690 million in 1976 to 4.321 million in 2000 to 7.878 million in 2012 (Institute of Education Sciences, 2014, Table 306.200).

Was NDSS in the vanguard of this trend, or did NDSS follow it? There is no way to know with any degree of certainty, but clearly the topics of the issues from 1997 through 2014 focused on addressing the needs of historically underrepresented students. These needs included not just issues related to race and ethnicity but also those of students with disabilities, students who were older than the traditional-aged college student, and veterans.

Sandeen and Barr (2006) observed that "identifying a previously ignored or unmet need of a group of students on the campus and then helping this group become an appreciated member of the campus community has been among the most important contributions that student affairs leaders had made to their institutions" (p. 57). Whether the *NDSS* volumes published from 1997 through 2014 have facilitated that work is unknown, but we can claim that we have released a number of volumes with that goal in mind.

Second, we speculate that the selection of titles reflects a maturing student affairs profession. That is, student affairs after World War II "grew phenomenally, both in the introduction of new programs and the expansion of old ones" (Rhatigan, 2009, pp. 12–13). The literature of the profession has evolved in the past few decades from articles, for example, that described promising administrative practices to analyzing student experiences and recommending approaches that student affairs educators could implement to enhance student learning. In short, the literature of student affairs over the last half of the 20th century evolved from articles that "explained how to do it" to examining "if the results of an experience led to student growth."

The content of the first 70 volumes, from the launch of *NDSS* in 1978 through issue 70 released in 1995, explored administrative topics such as budgeting, organization of student affairs, assessment of student affairs, and development of programs for students and so on. Our volumes explore these issues as well, but fully 67% of the earlier titles had these foci (in contrast to 48% of ours). We might posit that, in the first decade and a half of *NDSS*, concerns of student affairs educators tended to focus on providing services to students. That is, students would go to student affairs offices, or participate in various experiences overseen by student affairs administrators, that were designed as services or experiences in the cocurriculum (see Magolda & Quaye, 2011, pp. 388–389, for a further discussion on the evolution of the cocurriculum) for students.

A third possibility is that change in focus of the volumes was nothing more than happenstance. Although we, as editors, have been committed to dealing with topics that we thought would be interesting, useful, challenging, and timely, it is entirely possible that topics just emerged as random events rather than planned attempts to address current issues. We would rather not think so.

Conclusion

This look backward has, if nothing else, provided us with an opportunity to consider the decisions we have made over the past 2 decades as whole and see potential themes and trends in those decisions. We hope, however, that our retrospective—and our work as editors—provide a picture of the evolution of trends and literature in student affairs during a time of tremendous change in American higher education. We also intend the glance back to offer a context for the chapters that follow in this sourcebook.

References

Institute of Education Sciences. (2014). *Advance release of selected 2013 digest tables.* Washington, DC: U.S. Department of Education, National Center for Education Statistics. Retrieved from http://nces.ed.gov/programs/digest/2013menu_tables.asp

Komives, S. R., & Carpenter, S. (2009). Professional development as life-long learning. In G. S. McClellan, J. Stringer, & Associates (Eds.), *The handbook of student affairs administration* (3rd ed., pp. 371–387). San Francisco, CA: Jossey-Bass.

Magolda, P. M., & Quaye, S. J. (2011). Teaching in the co-curriculum. In J. H. Schuh, S. R. Harper, & S. R. Jones (Eds.), *Student services: A handbook for the profession* (6th ed., pp. 385–398). San Francisco, CA: Jossey-Bass.

Patton, L. D., & Harper, S. R. (2009). Using reflection to reframe theory-to-practice in student affairs. In G. S. McClellan, J. Stringer, & Associates (Eds.), *The handbook of student affairs administration* (3rd ed., pp. 147–165). San Francisco, CA: Jossey-Bass.

Pope, R. L., & Mueller, J. A. (2011). Multicultural competence. In J. H. Schuh, S. R. Harper, & S. R. Jones (Eds.), *Student services: A handbook for the profession* (6th ed., pp. 337–352). San Francisco, CA: Jossey-Bass.

Rhatigan, J. J. (2009). From the people up. In G. S. McClellan, J. Stringer, & Associates (Eds.), *The handbook of student affairs administration* (3rd ed., pp. 3–18). San Francisco, CA: Jossey-Bass.

Sandeen, A., & Barr, M. J. (2006). *Critical issues for student affairs.* San Francisco, CA: Jossey-Bass.

Snyder, T. D., & Dillow, S. A. (2013). *Digest of education statistics 2012* (NCES 2014-015). Washington, DC: U.S. Department of Education, Institute of Education Sciences, National Center for Education Statistics.

Wiley Online Library. (2014). *New Directions for Student Services.* Retrieved from http://onlinelibrary.wiley.com/journal/10.1002/%28ISSN%291536-0695/homepage /ProductInformation.html

ELIZABETH J. WHITT *is vice provost and dean for undergraduate education and professor of sociology at University of California, Merced.*

JOHN H. SCHUH *is director of the Emerging Leaders Academy and distinguished professor emeritus at Iowa State University.*

2

Four principal evolutions that have affected student affairs practice are identified and discussed in this chapter.

Trends and Milestones Affecting Student Affairs Practice

Florence A. Hamrick, Krista Klein

Higher education as well as the work of student affairs professionals in colleges and universities has evolved in recent years due in part to notable changes in the surrounding political, economic, and social contexts of higher education. In this chapter, we identify and discuss four principal evolutions that have had an impact on effective student affairs practice: (a) higher education cost and access; (b) student learning and development; (c) assessment and accountability; and (d) global engagement and sustainability.

As we planned this chapter, we also identified social justice and diversity and the rise of digital technologies and social media as "threads" that weave throughout this chapter and each of the selected topics. We know the four intersecting topics we selected will not cover the range of contemporary evolutions and events in the recent past that continue to shape the student affairs profession. Indeed, other chapters in this monograph address critically important and compelling events and developments. Our goal is to use these selected topics to help portray the changing, evolving nature of higher education that requires ongoing attention and reflection by practitioners and scholars to ensure the continued effectiveness, relevance, and responsiveness of student affairs in higher education.

Higher Education Cost and Access

The balance of federally subsidized student financial aid has shifted from grants to loans (e.g., Geiger & Heller, 2011), affecting both students' persistence to graduation and levels of debt for new graduates (Hossler, Ziskin, Gross, Kim, & Cekic, 2009). Cost reduction strategies have grown to include dual enrollment programs, online courses, and transfer of credits from lower cost institutions such as community colleges to baccalaureate degree-granting colleges and universities. To minimize or avoid debt, increasing numbers of students—including adult students—are employed at least part

NEW DIRECTIONS FOR STUDENT SERVICES, no. 151, Fall 2015 © 2015 Wiley Periodicals, Inc.
Published online in Wiley Online Library (wileyonlinelibrary.com) • DOI: 10.1002/ss.20134

time, with potentially negative implications for students' campus engagement and academic achievement (Pike, Kuh, & Massa-McKinley, 2009).

Rising costs of tuition, fees, and living expenses have significantly affected students' access to higher education and continue to influence the nature of many students' higher education experience. Even relatively small tuition increases affect enrollment numbers and credit hour production across public universities (Hemelt & Marcotte, 2011). Additionally, rounds of cumulative reductions—sometimes drastic reductions—in support for higher education at state levels often prompt corresponding rounds of tuition increases (Oliff, Palacios, Johnson, & Leachman, 2013).

Admissions processes that may curtail diversity of the student body are additional higher education access concerns, as are providing adequate and appropriate support for first-generation, low-income students in particular. Increasing numbers of students with diagnosed mental, emotional, or behavioral health conditions enroll in college. The numbers of students with disabilities continue to rise, as do requests for appropriate ADA (Americans with Disabilities Act) accommodations (Lee, 2014). The capacities of campus facilities and trained staff to serve students' needs—as well as relative levels of students' help-seeking and self-advocacy behaviors—are also of concern with respect to accessing higher education (Hunt & Eisenberg, 2010). Increasing numbers of campuses have established databases that enable early identification of students in potential academic difficulty as well as interdisciplinary campus teams to identify and assist students exhibiting behaviors that may place themselves or others at risk (National Behavioral Intervention Team Association, 2014).

Issues of higher education costs and access have direct implications for student affairs professionals. In light of reduced program-level resources, students increasingly pay fees to participate in, for example, new student orientation or cocurricular learning opportunities such as service trips over spring, fall, or winter breaks. For college students who are employed at least part time, their academic and work demands may reduce the balance of time and energy available for engagement in beneficial campus-based cocurricular opportunities. This situation may be particularly acute among students for whom college represents a major expense that cannot be fully underwritten by family members or through student financial assistance.

On the other hand, some of the difficulties associated with higher education access and cost have given rise to new waves of student activism and campus/community organizing. Along with recent campus and community protests of police actions or grand jury decisions that have received national if not international attention, student "Occupy" movements often focus disproportionately on high student debt attributable to student loans as well as access to employment opportunities that hold promise for economic stability and advancement. Undocumented students have also been at the forefront of organizing and lobbying in support of state and national "DREAM"

Acts (Development, Relief, and Education for Alien Minors); national immigration reform; and access to state, federal, and institutional student aid programs.

Another growing challenge for student affairs professionals is serving online students appropriately and effectively. Designing and offering "virtual student affairs" to advance the learning of students who are principally if not solely enrolled in online courses—including attention to enrolled students in other countries—provides a very important opportunity to enlarge both reach and impact on students by student affairs professionals.

Fostering Student Learning and Development

In the past 20 years, student learning and development has shifted to the forefront of student affairs practice, with the very definition of student learning being called into question. The increasing diversity of American college students with respect to age, gender, race, sexual orientation, and other characteristics is coupled with the external pressures of a global knowledge economy. Different types of students with differing priorities for attending college are also changing learning environments. In order to meet the demands of both students and the economy, student affairs practitioners must increase their knowledge base and their approaches to stay relevant. The influential 2004 report *Learning Reconsidered* challenged traditional student learning methods and argued that student affairs work will continue to change in response to trends in student demographics, student learning, and desired student outcomes (Keeling & Associates, 2004).

An increasingly diverse student body at colleges and universities contributes to a diverse learning environment with new outcomes of citizenship regarding understanding, appreciating, and respecting differences. Not only is citizenship growing in importance in the United States, but many student affairs educators also recognize the importance of creating global citizens across the world. Indeed, Greenhow and Robelia (2009) maintain that in order for students to remain academically successful in and outside of their college experience, they must develop 21st century competencies including technological fluency, innovation, and digital citizenship. Colleges and universities—and faculty and staff members in particular—are likely to vary widely with respect to formal and informal capacities to provide opportunities to develop these competencies. A document commonly known as the Spellings Report echoes the findings of *Learning Reconsidered* and advocates for a "greater emphasis on international education, including foreign language instructions and study abroad, in order to ensure that graduates have the skills necessary to function effectively in the global workforce" (U.S. Department of Education, 2006, p. 26). This global orientation has become a top priority for many higher education institutions today due to the globalizing economy and also because of an interest in graduating citizens with wide-ranging awareness, respect, dignity, and responsibility.

In order to meet these needs, student affairs staff must be willing to adapt their teaching and educational strategies to help students develop into global citizens while on campus and facilitate their subsequent transitions into the workforce. In *Take Back Higher Education*, Giroux and Giroux (2008) explained that colleges and universities should accept primary responsibility for developing students into adults who can actively participate in and critique the world beyond their institutions. At the same time, Heiberger and Harper (2008) noted, "just as students are multidimensional in their talents, interests, and abilities, so must student affairs staff members be creative in implementing programs that support these talents, interests, and abilities" (p. 32). New approaches and tools to facilitate student learning must be embraced by student affairs professionals in order to help students gain necessary competencies to realize future success and to build the future: "[U]niversities and colleges remain uniquely placed to prepare students to both understand and influence the larger educational forces that shape their lives" (Giroux & Giroux, 2008, p. 7). These learning environments range from experiential learning opportunities to online learning and cross-departmental collaborations to provide a liberal and humanistic education.

Promoting Unbounded Learning Environments

Learning Reconsidered speaks to the changes in student learning in recent years, focusing on the blended relationships of personal development with learning. Accordingly, the authors encourage student affairs professionals and programs to provide opportunities for students to "learn through action, contemplation, reflection, and emotional engagement as well as information acquisition" (Keeling & Associates, 2004, p. 12). This shift from traditional classroom learning to experience-based learning helps students to consider holistically the meanings of their college experiences, rather than limit "learning" to lecture halls and classrooms.

Giroux and Giroux (2008) noted that educators of all types must now create new discourses, pedagogical practices, and collective strategies to engage students: "[W]e [must] struggle to keep alive those institutional spaces, forums, and public spheres that support and defend critical education" (Giroux & Giroux, 2008, p. 9). While creating these spaces and spheres, student affairs professionals must encourage students to think critically and reflect on their learning and development through programming such as service-learning and social justice education. Collaborative efforts and connections between inside and out-of-classroom learning can have an even more significant impact on student learning. New organizational structures including student affairs have begun to appear, "especially centers, programs, and experimental collaborations that incorporate innovative learning methods ... to fit the needs of a particular campus and its students" (Keeling & Associates, 2004, p. 21), that aim to improve students' cultural competence and engagement with diverse people and perspectives.

Powerful learning environments include living and learning communities of various designs, credit-bearing service learning courses, and courses featuring experiential teaming and project success orientations, to name a few. Such opportunities are engaging students in active learning, which is one of the key principles of student affairs practice (Blimling, Whitt, & Associates, 1999). Active learning positions students as agents of their own learning and provides students with opportunities to reflect on their own experiences as well as others' perspectives. Similarly, the Spellings Report (U.S. Department of Education, 2006) advocated that "the needs of today's emerging generations of students require that our traditionally distinct categories of academic learning and student development be fused in an integrated, comprehensive vision of learning as a transformative process that is centered in and responsive to the whole student" (p. 30). Although these collaborations are widely considered essential, the numbers and effectiveness of collaborations must also grow in order to influence student learning.

In addition to structuring effecting collaborations and innovative learning environments on campus, the Spellings Report advocated for new learning paradigms including distance education, adult education, and workplace programs to broaden access to higher education and better accommodate the needs of an increasingly diverse student body. There are early indicators of success: Pascarella and Terenzini (2005) found that students who study via distance education learn as much as those students who learn in traditional classroom settings on campus. Student affairs professionals have also begun complementing traditional advising methods by adding social networking or information technology components. These integrated approaches provide different types of students with self-paced learning opportunities and information "on demand," which can accommodate students' increasingly busy schedules, especially for the growing population of adult learners (Kuh & Vesper, 1999). The findings of the Spellings Report indicate that promoting information technology in college learning environments improve "access, interaction, and sharing of educational materials from a variety of institutions, disciplines, and educational perspectives" (U.S. Department of Education, 2006, p. 25), thus creating a more well-rounded learning experience for students. Kuh and Vesper (1999) also found that technology can enhance student learning by permitting students to choose their own pace, enrich learning activities, and provide low-cost learning opportunities that can easily be balanced within students' busy schedules.

Harnessing this technology and using it in productive ways in student affairs settings is key. Pascarella and Terenzini (2005) indicated that, when used appropriately, visual media can facilitate meaning-making for students in a way that traditional lectures cannot. Effective use of visual media need not be limited to the classroom; student affairs professionals should also consider using videos or other online training tools in conjunction with campus programming and work with students. Pascarella and Terenzini showed that distance education does not disadvantage students—compared to their peers in on-campus classrooms—and that lecturing is a less effective method of teaching, even though it takes place in person. For those student affairs professionals at the forefront of creating and facilitating experiences for students, they can truly affect the "learning that occurs when students are actively engaged in processing information in new and personally relevant ways and, in a very real sense, constructing their own knowledge" (Pascarella & Terenzini, 2005, p. 101). For example, students' clarifications of identity and purpose via campus-based interactions, experiences, and reflection can be augmented by the personalized processing and learning that may occur on social media as students create, enact, and rework their digital identities and relationships.

Assessment and Accountability

As mentioned frequently throughout this chapter, several documents issued in the early 21st century identify a general lack of transparency on the part of colleges and universities when working with multiple constituents, including prospective students and families and current students. The Spellings Report (U.S. Department of Education, 2006) critiqued higher education rankings like those published by *U.S. News and World Report* for their emphasis on perceived reputation rather than actual performance. Misinformation or no information perpetuated—even unintentionally—by higher education institutions can contribute negatively to higher education access through inadequate academic preparation of students, lack of information about college opportunities, and understanding of the financial barriers and sources of financial support available for attending college.

In many ways foreshadowing current efforts in the federal government to "grade" colleges and universities, the report noted that parents have no evidence of how much students learn in college or whether they learn more at certain colleges. In discussing public education as a whole, Giroux and Giroux (2008) acknowledged that university students will have to deal with the consequences of the commercialization of higher education, including tuition increases, limited course offerings, and the rise of transactional models to describe many students' and parents' expectations of college. A focus on consumerism, branding, and marketing in higher education leads colleges and student affairs educators to offer highly desirable amenities like state-of-the-art fitness centers, modern student residence halls or apartments, as well as the ubiquitous climbing walls. However, rather than focusing on efforts to attract more and more students, the Spellings Report stated: "Higher education institutions should improve institutional cost management through the development of new performance benchmarks designed to measure and improve productivity and efficiency" (Keeling & Associates, 2006, p. 19). *Good Practice in Student Affairs* (Blimling, Whitt, & Associates, 1999) also emphasized documentation of student learning and benchmarking, which can itself be translated into competitive advantages for colleges and universities. Specifically, student performance should be articulated clearly to students, faculty, and staff, and regular assessment should take place to measure whether performance is consistent with institutional expectations. Implementing assessments of student learning as well as demonstrating responsible stewardship of resources in support of student learning have become common expectations for student affairs units and professionals in recent years.

Assessment in Student Affairs

In *Learning Reconsidered*, the commissioned authors urged that student affairs administrators at each institution should "determine and specify intended student outcomes and should commit resources to measuring, assessing, and documenting students' achievement of those outcomes" (Keeling & Associates, 2004, p. 28). For student affairs professionals, this means that the achievement of learning outcomes should serve as the primary consideration when determining resource expenditures. Blimling, Whitt, and Associates (1999) argued that the best student affairs professionals create learning environments that foster achievement of the institutions' outcomes for students. This includes using relevant theory and research to inform the creation and evaluation of educational programs and services. Student affairs must also go further by collaborating with other campus educators to create more effective, multifaceted educational environments and learning opportunities.

Student affairs professionals should initiate, or at least participate in, institution-wide conversations on student learning. According to Blimling, Whitt, and Associates (1999), student affairs educators are most successful when they set out to discover what students are learning from existing programs and services and determine ways to further enhance students' learning. Such an approach helps to create an environment of assessment and inquiry and values proactive research about students and their learning. Additionally, the authors explain that student affairs educators who are skilled in assessment techniques and use them regularly can evaluate results more quickly and are able to create new strategies to improve the environment or program as well as student learning. By advocating data-driven decision making and dynamic research-to-practice-to-research collaborations, student affairs educators assist their institutions in moving away from reputation-based to performance-based indicators of institutional quality, and ultimately improve the holistic learning environments for current and prospective students.

Although the importance of student affairs educators conducting assessment is stressed throughout the literature, practitioners should also consider what effective student performance looks like at their institutions. Expectations for student performance inside and outside of the classroom should be consistent with the institution's mission and related guiding documents, but expectations should also be set to a higher standard. According to Blimling, Whitt, and Associates (1999), while conducting assessments, student affairs practitioners should use systematic inquiry to address a wide range of student behaviors including academic achievement, intellectual and psychosocial development, and individual and community responsibility. Through shared understandings that learning takes many shapes and through viewing the campus holistically as a learning-centered environment, academics and student affairs professionals can collaborate more effectively and assess student learning as well as the relative successes of collaborative efforts.

Global Engagement and Sustainability

At many colleges and universities, September 11, 2001, and its aftermath have been accompanied by a range of outcomes, perceptions, and conclusions. For example, many students of Middle Eastern heritage were targets of anger and worse. Depending partly on the country of origin, securing student and faculty visas to the United States became an arduous process involving heightened scrutiny and much longer delays than before. A number of academics slated to serve as visiting scholars or researchers in the United States were prohibited from entering the country, and at least one faculty member of Middle Eastern descent was fired following a false accusation of funding terrorist activity.

Attention to risk management and potential liabilities for U.S. students and scholars traveling abroad was heightened, and State Department travel advisory warnings were carefully considered. Running estimates of vulnerabilities to future attacks—the National Terrorism Advisory System—were portrayed as green through red levels of alert. As fears and defensive stereotypes emerged, so did expressions of deeper and profound connectedness to the larger community. Rates of volunteerism and community service engagement by college students are high and continue to grow. The numbers of "Earth Day" and "Earth Week" celebrations in the United States and other countries have expanded since the first Earth Day in 1970 in the United States. Earth Day curricula in elementary and secondary schools are now commonplace, and refillable water bottles clipped to backpacks and bags have become common sights on campuses.

At some college campuses students take the lead in recycling and waste reduction programs, environmental protection initiatives, and living–learning communities centered on "green" housing, organic agriculture or gardening, and cultivating sustainable practices in everyday life. For example, Berea College in Kentucky recently opened a new "Deep Green" residence hall as a living/learning laboratory and also maintains an Ecovillage of apartments, shared community spaces, and gardens.

Many colleges and universities have expanded across the world via electronic access to coursework or, in some cases, brick-and-mortar campuses, often in collaboration with host countries including China and the United Arab Emirates. Students can access sources of news and information across the world via social media or web-based providers and in some cases have organized or participated in social movements that are linked electronically, such as the "Occupy" movements that emerged in a number of countries. Blogs, Facebook, and Twitter enable students to play an integral role in spreading news, developments, and reports—for better and for worse, depending on the source. Additionally, most published journals and books are available online, and sites like Wikipedia seek to "democratize" knowledge via crowd sourcing and collaboration.

Conclusions and Recommendations

From this exploration, we draw three principal conclusions with associated recommendations for practice.

First, it is clear that student "engagement" is no longer limited to campus-based, campus-related, or campus-sanctioned involvements. Because of other life commitments and/or engagement in political, social, or economic movements, students' opportunities for learning are vast and not necessarily overseen or provided by student affairs professionals—or by faculty members. What student affairs professionals can provide are validation and opportunities for reflection and learning. This work will entail professionals following *students'* leads and taking the initiative to learn even more about the students with whom they work. For example, student affairs professionals might not (or might!) take part in campus activism or protest activities, but they can validate participating students as engaged citizens and help students mine those experiences for insights and learning.

Related to this point, student affairs professionals should realize that potential "learning environments" for students are numerous and encompass electronic media and social media in particular. Social media apps permit expanding networks of "friendships" and relationships through which students may grow and develop in ways that complement face-to-face interactions and relationships. The size of students' learning environments is broad if not boundless once electronic media and social media are affirmed as learning environments in which powerful growth and learning can occur. Whether and how student affairs professionals and units operate in this expanded environment—with the goals of advancing student learning—is a work in progress. Additionally, for example, ethically appropriate professional behaviors may require reviewing as professionals engage students via electronic and social media, and to help students engage each other respectfully and appropriately. The final conclusion is related to the first two. Student affairs continues to professionalize through, for example, dedicated graduate degree programs as well as formal adoption and dissemination of levels and types of competencies for professionals. Discussions of credentialing and certification for student affairs also continue. The profession of student affairs indeed continues to evolve, and continued professional and educational development is necessary to meet the challenges of those evolutions. In light of reduced institutional resources, many more professional development programs and networking opportunities are offered online (e.g., webinars and online educational or training modules). Additionally, groups of student affairs professionals design and structure popular professional development opportunities for themselves (e.g., #SAChat) in a form of crowdsourcing and sharing in virtual space.

As the profession has evolved, the need for student affairs *professionals* to evolve in terms of learning, creativity, and adaptability is greater than ever.

References

Blimling, G. S., Whitt, E. J., & Associates. (1999). *Good practice in student affairs: Principles to foster student learning.* San Francisco, CA: Jossey-Bass.

Geiger, R. L., & Heller, D. E. (2011). *Financial trends in higher education: The United States* (Working Paper No. 6). University Park, PA: Pennsylvania State University, Center for the Study of Higher Education.

Giroux, H. A., & Giroux, S. S. (2008). *Take back higher education: Race, youth, and the crisis of democracy in the post-civil rights era.* New York, NY: Macmillan.

Greenhow, C., & Robelia, B. (2009). Informal learning and identity formation in online social networks. *Learning, Media, and Technology, 34*(2), 119–140.

Heiberger, G., & Harper, R. (2008). Have you Facebooked Astin lately? Using technology to increase student involvement. In R. Junco & D. M. Timm (Eds.), *New Directions for Student Services: No. 124. Using emerging technologies to enhance student engagement* (pp. 19–35). San Francisco, CA: Jossey-Bass.

Hemelt, S. W., & Marcotte, D. E. (2011). The impact of tuition increases on enrollment at public colleges and universities. *Educational Evaluation and Policy Analysis, 33*(4), 435–457.

Hossler, D., Ziskin, M., Gross, J. P. K., Kim, S., & Cekic, O. (2009). Student aid and its role in encouraging persistence. In J. C. Smart (Ed.), *Higher education: Handbook of theory and research* (Vol. 24). New York, NY: Springer.

Hunt, J., & Eisenberg, D. (2010). Mental health problems and help-seeking behavior among college students. *Journal of Adolescent Health, 46*(1), 3–10.

Keeling, R. P., & Associates. (2004). *Learning reconsidered: A campus-wide focus on the student experience.* Washington, DC: National Association of Student Personnel Administrators and American College Personnel Association.

Kuh, G. D., & Vesper, N. (1999, April). *Do computers enhance or detract from student learning?* Paper presented at the meeting of the American Educational Research Association, Montreal, Canada.

Lee, B. A. (2014). Students with disabilities: Opportunities and challenges for colleges and universities. *Change*, 46(1), 40–45.

National Behavioral Intervention Team Association. (2014). *Behavioral intervention teams*. Retrieved from https://nabita.org/behavioral-intervention-teams/

Oliff, P., Palacios, V., Johnson, I., & Leachman, M. (2013, March 19). *Recent deep state higher education cuts may harm students and the economy for years to come*. Washington, DC: Center on Budget and Policy Priorities.

Pascarella, E. T., & Terenzini, P. T. (2005). *How college affects students: A third decade of research*. San Francisco, CA: Jossey-Bass.

Pike, G. R., Kuh, G. D., & Massa-McKinley, R. C. (2009). First-year students' employment, engagement, and academic achievement: Untangling the relationship between work and grades. *Journal of Student Affairs Research and Practice*, 45(4), 1012–1034.

U.S. Department of Education. (2006). *A test of leadership: Charting the future of U.S. Higher Education*. Washington, DC: Author.

FLORENCE A. HAMRICK is professor in the Graduate School of Education at Rutgers University.

KRISTA KLEIN is assistant director of new student orientation and family programs at Rutgers University.

3

Undergraduate students have changed over the past 20 years. This chapter traces the evolution of students, reviews effective student affairs responses, and considers practice moving forward.

Characterizations of Students and Effective Student Affairs Practice

Jillian Kinzie

Students are the center of student affairs practice. Who undergraduate students are, what they need, what they experience in college, who they are to become, and what they gain from higher education are all prime concerns of student affairs professionals. A strong student-oriented perspective drives the profession and informs the design of programs and services to enhance student development and the creation of learning environments that support student success. As the chief caretakers of the whole student, student affairs professionals must understand evolving student needs and know how to integrate this information into effective student affairs practice.

Fortunately, quarterly monographs in the *New Directions for Student Services* (*NDSS*) series provide a wealth of timely research on undergraduate students to inform student affairs practice. Tracing conceptions of undergraduate students beginning in 1996, through the 20 years that John Schuh and Elizabeth Whitt served as *NDSS* editors, is an intriguing way to consider the evolutions of students and the implications for student affairs practice. This chapter discusses how conceptions of students have changed from 1996 to 2015, synthesizes the implications for student affairs practice, and closes with considerations for effective student affairs practice moving forward.

Conceptions of Undergraduate Students Over Time

Since the founding of U.S. colleges, there has been plenty of discussion about undergraduate students, the lives they lead on campus, and what this means to college and university administrators. More than 100 years ago, college students were privileged young men who engaged in courses in classical languages, religion, and philosophy that demanded recitations and a structured learning environment. The increase in college enrollments and

NEW DIRECTIONS FOR STUDENT SERVICES, no. 151, Fall 2015 © 2015 Wiley Periodicals, Inc.
Published online in Wiley Online Library (wileyonlinelibrary.com) • DOI: 10.1002/ss.20135

sports after World War I, and in the 1920s, of parties, gin, and gambling, created livelier student environments. The GI Bill spurred significant enrollment growth, dramatically changed student activities, and influenced more students to major in science and technology, and the 20th century phenomenon of the diversification of the student body ushered in new practices emphasizing inclusion. This brief snapshot of undergraduate students over the last 100 years illustrates significant changes in the characterizations of students.

Higher education scholars, demographers, economists, historians, sociologists, the popular press, and others have produced a range of descriptions of undergraduate students over time. As a species, undergraduate students have been classified based on their demographic characteristics, values and attitudes, habits and behaviors, and generational patterns, and this information has been used by higher education policymakers and by those who work directly with students. Demographic data, for instance, about high school graduates combined with observations about the women's movement foretold the increase in the enrollment of women in higher education. Similarly, upon discovering that the views of entering students between 1967 and 1974 were increasingly in greater support of student autonomy and rights and less supportive of institutional control over student publications and controversial speakers (Astin, 1998), some campus educators modified restrictive policies governing student rights and campus events. Characterizations of undergraduates provide a comprehensive view of students, are useful for informing higher education policymaking, and can help campus educators know how to foster student growth and anticipate challenges. However, because characterizations change over time, they reveal one thing for certain: no matter the time period, students are different from their counterparts of the last decade (Horowitz, 2013). Characterizations of undergraduate students are important to understanding students and determining implications for student affairs practice. To organize a summary of how students have been represented over the last 20 years, I discuss six broad categories for describing undergraduate students: (a) demographic trends, (b) sociohistorical context, (c) generational perspective, (d) student attitudes and values, (e) assessment of student experiences, and (f) student development research and student needs.

Demographic Trends.   Demographic information about high school graduates, who students are upon entry to college, and differences in who persists and completes college is fundamental information about undergraduate students. The U.S. Department of Education's annual Condition of Education report summarizes important trends in education and indicators of the basic characteristics of undergraduates. Over the last 20 years, demographic data show that historically underrepresented racial-ethnic groups (for example, African American and Latino students) made significant gains in access to higher education. Postsecondary education also started serving more students aged 28 and older than traditional-age students. More recent demographic information indicates rising numbers of international and undocumented students making their way into U.S. institutions. These demographic shifts have resulted in expanded policies and programming responsive to these populations of students. Above all, over the last dozen years, data indicating slow progress in increasing college completion rates overall and serious graduation rate gaps have resulted in greater emphasis in improving the conditions for college student success. Shifting student demographic information and, in particular, concern about inequities in college completion have prompted greater attention by student affairs professionals to monitor retention and graduation rates, address differences by race-ethnicity and socioeconomic status, and implement initiatives to address student persistence and improve student success.

Sociohistorical Context. Conceptions of undergraduate students influenced by societal and historical context reveals more overarching characteristics of students. Over the last 20 years, the most significant contextual issue shaping college students includes the failure of federal and state financial aid to keep up with the cost of college and reductions in financial assistance. This has resulted in significant student and family concerns about financing college. More recently, the recession of 2008 made it difficult for college graduates to get jobs and contributed to more students returning home after graduation to live with their parents. Less student financial assistance, and increased reliance on college loans, led student affairs professionals to emphasize educating students about financial assistance, including how to manage debt, and resulted in greater sensitivity to students' financial situation and stress.

The societal or cultural conditions that students have experienced are also a clear way to characterize students. For example, since 1998, the Beloit College Mindset List (see www.beloit.edu/mindset) has identified the cultural touchstones that have shaped the worldview of students entering colleges and universities. As a catalog of the changing perceptions of new students, it signals important shifts in students' awareness of AIDS, knowledge about the Cold War, the role of technology, and more recently, the influence of social media. This popular list serves as a reminder to student affairs educators to be wary of dated references and also to appreciate students' experiences as they transition to college. Undoubtedly, the most significant influence on students over the last 20 years is the increasing role of technology and the ubiquity of the Internet and social media.

Generational Perspective. Characterizations of undergraduate students by generational attributes are popular ways to depict students. The generation in college between 1996 and 2015, "the millennial generation" (students born from the early 1980s to the early 2000s), has been ascribed the traits of civic-mindedness, confidence, and tolerance, but also a sense of entitlement and narcissism (Howe & Strauss, 2000; Twenge, 2006). Millennials, for example, are characterized as achievement oriented, focused on getting good grades and seeking awards, and inclined to view their college education as a commodity or entitlement. These characterizations have influenced student affairs practitioners to, for example, focus attention on helping students understand more specifically what they have learned in their academic and leadership achievements (for example, public speaking, critical thinking); they have also adopted more intentional approaches to persuade students to engage more fully in and out of the classroom (Crone & MacKay, 2007). Even more consideration has been given to millennial students' more regular contact with parents to consult on minor decisions. In response, student affairs employed the students' relationship with their family to reinforce the priority of learning and started enlisting family members' help by educating them about campus resources.

Student Attitudes and Values.   Tracking student attitudes, values, interests, and experiences has become an increasingly more sophisticated way to describe and understand undergraduate students. New student information from surveys like The Freshman Survey administered by the Higher Education Research Institute (HERI) has provided a snapshot of what incoming students are like, including information about students' probable careers, reasons for attending college, and life goals. These conceptions have, for example, been used by campus activities programmers to identify speakers or events likely to be attractive to students and by career advisors to anticipate the kinds of careers or internship opportunities that students might desire. For example, in 1997, new students were reported to be the most community-service-minded class in the 31-year history of The Freshman Survey (Sax, Astin, Korn, & Mahoney, 1996); this trait helped usher in an emphasis on community service and service-learning activities in student life. Another attitude that shifted over this period is respect for diversity and in students' assertion that all their heritages should be respected, counted, and acknowledged. In student affairs, this shift emphasized the importance of expanded services in multicultural centers, greater integration of students with disabilities, and an increase in social justice programming.

Assessment of Student Experiences.   Assessing what undergraduates do, how they spend their time, and the effort they expend on activities that matter for learning and development is another way to represent undergraduate students. The qualities of undergraduate students' experiences have been demonstrated in results from the College Student Experience Questionnaire, the College Student Survey (CSS), and since 2000, the National Survey of Student Engagement (NSSE). Student affairs practitioners have learned from the CSS that, in general, students are satisfied with their college experiences. Yet, despite the fact that students were participating in honors courses and taking advantage of study-abroad opportunities, as well as participating in leadership and cocurricular activities, some students still report being bored and showing up late to class at least some of the time, which suggests some student disengagement relative to educational responsibilities (Saenz & Barrera, 2007). Similarly, NSSE (2004) highlighted that first-year students at liberal arts colleges spent an average of nearly 7 hours per week on cocurricular activities versus just a little more than 4 hours at master's colleges and universities (defined as "institutions that awarded at least 50 master's degrees and fewer than 20 doctoral degrees during the year"; see http://carnegieclassifications.iu.edu/descriptions/basic.php). More concerning, NSSE results revealed that only about 11% of full-time students spent more than 25 hours a week preparing for class, the approximate number that faculty members say is needed to do well in college. These results have helped student affairs professionals identify areas of improvement in the undergraduate experience, devise approaches to reach students through cocurricular activities and instruction, and anticipate habits that could benefit from intervention.

Student Development Research and Student Needs. Research and theories about undergraduate student development are perhaps the most significant conceptualization of students for student affairs practice. Over the last 20 years student development research has expanded to include more complex theories of psychosocial and identity development and models for spiritual and cognitive development. Identity development theories greatly expanded to include multiracial students, bisexual and transgendered students, and frameworks of intersectionality. Related to the category of research about student development is the growing body of information characterizing undergraduate student needs and challenges. Information about undergraduate students' academic preparation, factors that make them at risk of dropping out, and more recently, research about the status of students' mental and emotional health have grown in significance in recent years. One of the growing student issues on campuses across the country is the increase in demand for personal counseling to address students' psychological and emotional needs. Corresponding to students' growing mental health needs, declining economic conditions in the mid-2000s elevated students' concern about their ability to find jobs, placing increased demands on career services and other postcollege transition and support programs.

Characterizations of undergraduate students are important to understanding who students are and what they experience in college at a particular point in time. A combination of the aforementioned categories provides a more comprehensive picture of undergraduate students and can help guide student affairs practice and ensure responsiveness to changing students' characteristics and needs.

Looking Back at the Emphasis on Students

A look back at the themes featured in the last 20 years of *NDSS* volumes reflects all of the aforementioned conceptions of students. Volume themes between 1996 and 1999 illustrate the strong influence of demographic, sociohistorical, and generational shifts in students as evidenced in titles addressing emerging concerns about student persistence in college, creating a commitment to inclusiveness, and appropriate implementation of affirmative action practices given increased student diversity and legal challenges to race-based approaches to achieving diversity. The complicated interplay between rising college costs and the use of financial aid to meet both student needs and campus enrollment goals was also reflected in the series. A volume on students with disabilities emphasized how to help students gain meaningful access and full participation in campus activities and an issue on African American male students documented the status of Black male college students and their attitudes, beliefs, and perceptions of the campus environment. These volumes aimed to help student affairs professionals understand their role in promoting student retention, advance inclusion practices and diversity to create a positive educational environment, and negotiate the complex relationship between student aid and enrollment management.

This period also reflects the intentional emphasis from student development and assessment research on the need to create effective learning environments and experiences for students and for this to be a central purpose of the student affairs profession. Volumes on cognitive development provided a theoretical framework on which to base intentional interventions and activities to create conditions for students to expend time and energy on educationally purposeful activities. Correspondingly, an issue on powerful programming for student learning provided guidance on implementing programming focused on learning and outcome evaluation and emphasized the importance of collaborating with faculty.

The topic of changing student demographics combined with the burgeoning number of racial and ethnic identity models related to specific groups—such as Latinos, Asians, and Native Americans and gay, lesbian, and bisexual students—was strongly represented in NDSS volumes between 2001 through 2011. Themes including working with Asian American students, meeting the special needs of adult students, veteran students, gender identity and sexual orientation, serving Native American students, addressing the unique needs of Latino students, and African American women illustrate the strong emphasis on advancing understanding of changing student demographics and the role of theory. Importantly, these volumes provided much needed examples of the application of advanced student development theories to student affairs practice to enrich understanding of college students' experiences and inform interventions to facilitate and enhance the development of diverse students.

Generational trends and current student issues are also reflected in the 20 years of NDSS volumes. Serving the millennial generation was a specific volume theme, and other volumes incorporated generational issues including the changing role of parents, students' increased expectations for digital technology, and interest in civic learning. A few volumes also covered current important topics such as student mental health, campus safety, and financial concerns. A campus safety volume, for example, encompassed perennial themes such as hazing and town–gown relations but also addressed the evolving nature of campus safety including parental partnerships, safety abroad, technology safety and security, and large-scale crisis response to campus tragedies. Concerns about financing student affairs and ensuring equity in opportunity so that programs and services for students survive and thrive was addressed in several issues.

In general, a review of the emphasis on students in *NDSS* over the last 20 years demonstrates persistent and significant attention to representing and understanding students who have been historically underserved in higher education and to providing resources to guide student affairs professionals in their efforts to serve these important student populations and create more inclusive learning environments. Corresponding with this movement is a greater focus on applying advanced student development theory and attending to demographic data to increase overall student success rates. Tracing the emphasis on students also reveals the prevalence of specific concerns including mental health, parental involvement, campus safety, and finances.

Changing Student Characteristics and Effective Student Affairs Responses

Changing student characteristics over the last 2 decades have stimulated important shifts in student affairs practice. By far, the most significant shifts are associated with the increased diversity among undergraduate students. Responses include the development of a broader portrait of the college-going student population and increased understanding of who students are, what they experience in college, and what they need to reach their educational goals. Differentiating services to reach for example, growing Latino, veteran, and transfer student populations, and to more effectively address the needs of students with disabilities via universal design, and so on, demonstrate effective responses to changing student characteristics. In particular, responsive campuses invested in what matters to Black male student success, including precollege preparatory opportunities, leadership development, financial aid, on-campus employment, and support and enrichment via Black student unions, undergraduate chapters of the National Society of Black Engineers, and other ethnic student groups (Harper, 2012). Without a doubt, the most effective responses to changing student demographic characteristics have been increased advocacy for inclusive environments and the development of more culturally responsive programming and services. In addition, the emphasis on multicultural education and social justice programming has appropriately expanded the educational benefits of diversity to all undergraduate students.

NEW DIRECTIONS FOR STUDENT SERVICES • DOI: 10.1002/ss

Exploring the topic of students over time also revealed a persistent concern about addressing issues of quality in undergraduate education. Several *NDSS* volumes suggested the importance of implementing assessment in student affairs in response to greater demand for evidence of educational quality and assessment. With a robust portfolio of assessment activities, the value of services, programs, and activities of a student affairs division can be confirmed. For example, assessment activities showcasing collaborative assessment initiatives involving academic and student affairs, or specifying policies or programs that enhance student persistence, and results demonstrating the value of multicultural programs on students' openness to diversity are effective responses to the emphasis on assessment and accountability. Overall, the emphasis on ensuring educational quality and evidence of effectiveness spurred the specification of outcomes and increased assessment activities in student affairs. On the related theme of greater attention to student learning, the publication of volumes on the topic of peer education suggests the growing importance of investing in practices that prioritize student learning.

Changing conditions in the student experience demonstrate the importance of applying theory and evidence-based practice to contemporary issues. The shooting tragedy on the campus of Virginia Tech, for example, refocused attention on students who struggle with serious mental health problems and are also dangerous and demonstrated the need for implementing emergency response and preparedness systems. Campuses responded by recommitting to evidence-based practice for prevention or treatment and implemented group dialogue and support programs to foster campus healing. Campuses also implemented tested processes for effective emergency response, enhanced communication technologies to notify the community and improve mobilization of emergency resources and first responders, expanded weapons regulations, increased mental health counseling, and developed new approaches to share concerning information with parents, medical professionals, and law enforcement agencies.

Finally, the concern of traditional-age undergraduate students about gaining practical skills and entering the workforce during uncertain economic conditions elevated their interest in internships, real-world experiences, and selecting majors with the most job opportunities. Financial stress and college affordability fears prompted the development of financial literacy programs through financial aid offices and first-year experience programs and in information for parents. Effective student affairs practice associated with these students, and their hovering parents' concerns, also included earlier emphasis on career advising, fostering student involvement in field experiences, internships, and leadership development programs to satisfy students' interest in gaining experience and demonstrable skills. Even more, responsive orientation and first-year program experiences and academic advisors picked up on student and family concerns and frontloaded career information, highlighted services and useful experiences, and outlined clear paths to foster timely degree progress and student success.

Looking Forward: Undergraduates and Implications for Student Affairs Practice

With nearly 20 million undergraduate students at the center of student affairs practice today, and goals for the number of distance education, adult, and transfer students to increase, there are in fact a lot of students to be concerned about. Student affairs will be increasingly expected to develop responsive services and programs for a wider range of students than today. One incontrovertible fact that the demographic, sociohistorical context, assessment, and developmental information on college students confirms is that students are not a monolithic group (Astin, 1998). Students will continue to participate in higher education in various ways, be more diverse, and bring a range of attitudes, beliefs, and experiences to college. Understanding who these students are when they enter college; characterizing them as individuals, cohorts, or generations and in sub-populations; and knowing their expectations and what they do while in college will be key to developing relevant services and programming.

The joint pressures of needing more diverse students than ever to complete postsecondary credentials and to do so under constrained financial conditions make it incumbent on student affairs professionals to leverage research and assessment data about college impact and student success to improve the conditions for completion. Decades of college impact research show that what students experience and gain from college varies among students, even those at the same institution, and that the effects of college are largely conditional, contingent on student characteristics including gender, race-ethnicity, and socioeconomic status and what students do in college. This research reinforces the need for student affairs professionals to stay current on research about growing student populations, maintain sensitivity to understanding these populations, attend to individual student needs, design inclusive environments, and implement programs and services that make educationally purposeful practices inescapable to thereby ensure success for all. Even more, the increase in completion and success rates can be achieved only through greater collaboration between student and academic affairs.

Another current and future reality is the variability in how students participate in college and earn postsecondary credentials. In addition to expanded distance or online education, it is clear that students will be earning college credits while still enrolled in high school, attending multiple institutions, or taking courses online and face-to-face simultaneously, leading to increased fragmentation of the college experience. Many college students already juggle multiple demands, greater financial burden, employment, and family obligations, and these conditions will further complicate efforts to ensure a cohesive experience and increase completion rates. These new realities will surely affect what can be achieved in orientation and first-year experience programs, approaches to student involvement in cocurricular programming and experiences, and the overall cohesiveness of an under-graduate education. The increasingly fragmented conditions of going to col-lege must be taken into account by student affairs professionals.

Undergraduates will also need to be better prepared to enter an econ-omy defined by greater workplace challenges and dynamism (Carnevale, Smith, & Strohl, 2010). In addition, our growing global economy puts more pressure on students to develop more sophisticated proficiencies in global understanding and learning. Students will need to develop broad, cross-cutting capacities for future career success. Student affairs will need to part-ner with academic affairs to more intentionally provide students opportu-nities to develop global understanding and diverse perspectives, apply their skills in different contexts, and create experiences to enrich global and civic learning.

The need for specialized care and education for undergraduate stu-dents at the turn of the 20th century was the impetus for the profession. Not surprisingly, the core value of being student oriented and emphasis on the notion that the whole student must be considered in every educational endeavor should persist. In fact, this emphasis and the sensitivity that stu-dent affairs professionals have to individual student needs should serve the future of student affairs well. Furthermore, the expanded emphasis on en-suring college completion and success for more students will place greater demands on all campus educators to attend to completion goals. Thankfully, the past 20 years of *NDSS* volumes position student affairs to continue to strive to make students' experience in college meaningful, supportive, de-velopmental, enriching, and transformative.

References

Astin, A. W. (1998). The changing American college student: Thirty-year trends, 1966–1996. *The Review of Higher Education, 21*, 115–135.

Carnevale, A. P., Smith, N., & Strohl, J. (2010, June). *Help wanted: Projec-tions of jobs and education requirements through 2018.* Washington, DC: George-town University, Center on Education and the Workforce. Retrieved from https://cew.georgetown.edu/report/help-wanted/

Crone, I., & MacKay, K. (2007). Motivating today's college students. *Peer Review, 9*(1), 18–21. Washington, DC: Association of American Colleges and Universities.

Harper, S. R. (2012). *Black male student success in higher education: A report from the Na-tional Black Male College Achievement Study.* Philadelphia: University of Pennsylvania, Center for the Study of Race and Equity in Education.

Horowitz, H. L. (2013). *Campus life.* New York, NY: Knopf.

Howe, N., & Strauss, W. (2000). *Millennials rising: The next great generation.* New York, NY: Random House.

National Survey of Student Engagement (NSSE). (2004). *Student engagement: Pathways to collegiate success.* Bloomington: Indiana University, Center for Postsecondary Research.

Saenz, V., & Barrera, R. (2007). *Findings from the 2005 College Student Survey (CSS): National aggregates.* Los Angeles: University of California, Higher Education Research Institute.

Sax, L. J., Astin, A. W., Korn, W. S., & Mahoney, K. M. (1996). *The American freshman: National norms for fall 1996.* Los Angeles: University of California, Higher Education Research Institute.

Twenge, J. (2006). *Generation me.* New York, NY: Free Press.

JILLIAN KINZIE *is associate director of the Center for Postsecondary Research, Indiana University School of Education.*

This chapter reviews the history and current state of assessment in student affairs. It evaluates our progress to date and makes recommendations for the future.

Looking Back and Ahead: What We Must Learn From 30 Years of Student Affairs Assessment

Becki Elkins

It has been nearly 25 years since T. Dary Erwin (1991) called on student affairs professionals to assume an active role in student assessment in higher education. Nearly 20 years have passed since Lee Upcraft and John Schuh (1996) urged student affairs to use assessment to "demonstrate its central role in the academic success of students" (p. 9). A proliferation of articles, books, presentations, and conferences focused on the "why" and "how" of student affairs assessment followed these calls. Decades later, one might see these items and wonder if we have reached the pinnacle of student assessment in student affairs. Is our work here done, so to speak? What remains? This chapter (a) briefly reviews the history of assessment, in general, and in student affairs in particular, (b) critically examines the role assessment plays—and does not play—in our work today, and (c) raises questions about and makes recommendations for the future of student affairs.

History of Assessment in Student Affairs

The modern era of assessment in higher education is rooted in the appeals for educational reform that emerged in the 1980s. Simultaneous calls by external organizations and state governments for curricular reform and institutional accountability for student learning began to transform the higher education landscape (Ewell, 2002). The release of two major reports on the state of higher education (National Governors' Association, 1986; National Institute for Education, 1984) resulted in two prominent driving forces that exerted demands for student learning and outcomes assessment—one based in institutional improvement, the other based in external accountability (Ewell, 2002).

New Directions for Student Services, no. 151, Fall 2015 © 2015 Wiley Periodicals, Inc.
Published online in Wiley Online Library (wileyonlinelibrary.com) • DOI: 10.1002/ss.20136

The First National Conference on Assessment in Higher Education took place in 1985 and was cosponsored by the National Institute of Education and the American Association for Higher Education (AAHE) (Ewell, 2002). Seven years later, the AAHE Assessment Forum released a statement on the principles of good practice for assessing student learning (Astin et al., 1992). The authors noted that assessment worked best when, among other things, student learning was recognized as multidimensional and integrated and when members across the educational community, including student affairs staff, were involved in its implementation.

Indeed, at approximately the same time as the AAHE principles were released, calls began to emerge for student affairs divisions and professionals to take an active role in student learning assessment (American College Personnel Association [ACPA], 1994; Erwin, 1991; Upcraft & Schuh, 1996). Erwin (1991) noted that student affairs traditionally had not been involved in assessing student learning but suggested that the assessment movement provided an opportunity to more clearly articulate what cocurricular experiences and environments contributed to student learning and development. The demands to shift to a student-centered learning paradigm (ACPA, 1994; Barr & Tagg, 1995) expanded opportunities for student affairs to demonstrate its centrality to the educational mission. *The Student Learning Imperative* (ACPA, 1994), followed, a decade later, by *Learning Reconsidered* (ACPA & National Association of Student Personnel Administrators [NASPA], 2004), implored student affairs professionals to take active responsibility for student learning, as opposed to limiting their role to the provision of services and programs. Assessment, argued Upcraft and Schuh (1996), provided a way for student affairs to make clear the connection between "our work" and the "academic mission of our institutions" (p. 12). Without demonstrating the central role it played in the academic success of students, the authors argued that student affairs would be left otherwise to "intuition, moral imperatives, good will, or serendipity to justify its existence" (p. 12).

Assessment literature in higher education, generally, and student affairs, specifically, proliferated over the next 2 decades. Resources ranged from the philosophical underpinnings and scholarship of assessment (e.g., Banta, 2002; Ewell, 2009) to practical guides for creating assessment plans (e.g., Schuh & Upcraft, 2001; Suskie, 2009), case studies highlighting effective implementation (e.g., Banta, 2004; Bresciani, Moore Gardner, & Hickmott, 2009a), and strategies for improving assessment efforts (e.g., Palomba & Banta, 1999). Authors argued for student affairs professionals to articulate and assess student learning outcomes (e.g., Bresciani et al., 2009b), develop "cultures of assessment" (e.g., Barham, Tschepikow, & Seagraves, 2013; Schuh, 2013), and assist their institutions in addressing issues of accountability by assuming active roles in the accreditation process (e.g., Allen, Elkins, Henning, Bayless, & Gordon, 2013).

As the turn of the 21st century took hold, student affairs professionals increasingly were expected to possess knowledge, skills, and competencies in assessment as a foundational piece of their educational training and professional development (ACPA, 2007; ACPA & NASPA, 2009). Graduate preparation programs began to incorporate assessment and program evaluation courses into their curricula. The two leading student affairs professional organizations—American College Personnel Association and National Association of Student Personnel Administrators—offered subgroups for members interested in assessment and evaluation. Although one such group, the ACPA Commission for Assessment and Evaluation, had been in existence since the 1960s, in the changing environment it shifted its emphasis from serving as a testing and survey warehouse for members to helping practitioners develop the knowledge, skills, and abilities necessary to conduct sound assessment of student learning. Organizations devoted to the assessment of student learning (e.g., Association for the Assessment of Learning in Higher Education, Association for Higher Education Effectiveness, National Institute for Learning Outcomes Assessment) and conferences and institutes designed to expand faculty and staff skills in assessment exploded in number (e.g., ACPA Student Affairs Assessment Institute, NASPA Assessment and Persistence Conference, Assessment Conference at Indiana University Purdue University at Indianapolis, Texas A&M University Assessment Conference).

Over this same period, many institutions developed assessment offices, often in the school's student affairs division (Livingston & Zerulik, 2013). These offices were staffed by institutional researchers and student affairs professionals with expertise in assessment, evaluation, and research methods. Malaney (1997) first examined the prevalence and function of what he identified as "student affairs research offices" (p. 2), noting that only 35 such offices existed. In 2007, ACPA and NASPA conducted a survey of assessment professionals in student affairs, identifying 77 individuals whose position titles fit the description (Elling & Bentrim, 2013). The Student Affairs Assessment Leaders (SAAL) organization was founded in 2008, with membership limited to those individuals whose positions devoted at least 50% of time and effort to student affairs assessment work. In its first year, SAAL membership included 40 student affairs professionals. By 2013, that number had grown to 233 professionals whose daily work encompassed commitment to student affairs assessment (Elling & Bentrim, 2013).

With this myriad of resources in place, Swing and Coogan, in 2010, announced that "assessment in postsecondary education [had] come of age" (p. 5). They highlighted increased depth in assessment and institutional research conferences as well as expanded tools for data collection, analysis, and reporting. Given this proliferation of written resources, professional organizations, and training and professional development opportunities as well as the rapid growth in numbers of student affairs assessment professionals (Elling & Bentrim, 2013), we might be tempted to make similar claims about learning outcomes assessment in student affairs. Would we be correct? Have we arrived? What is the current state of assessment in student affairs?

Current State of Assessment in Student Affairs

Two arenas illustrate the current state of student affairs assessment: a discussion of the stages of acceptance of assessment as part of our work and evidence of student learning outcomes assessment in student affairs.

Stages of Assessment.   Evaluating the progression of student learning assessment in higher education, Miller (2012) posited that the assessment movement mirrored Kübler-Ross's (1997) stages of grief: denial, anger, bargaining, depression, and acceptance. She reviewed the content and tone of articles published in *Change* between 1986 and 2011 to demonstrate higher education's response to the internal and external demands for student outcomes assessment. Miller concluded that higher education had "generally passed through the stages of grief into something like acceptance—acceptance of the need to examine our practices and to communicate about and use the results" (p. 8). She tempered that claim, however, noting that institutions continued to struggle with such challenges as articulating common learning outcomes, making evidence-based decisions, and publicly reporting assessment results.

The stages of assessment offered by Miller (2012) varied only slightly from those offered by Erwin (1991) at the beginning of the modern assessment movement. Erwin identified five stages of reaction to assessment: discovery, questioning, resistance, participation, and commitment. Discovery entails first learning about assessment and is characterized by reading articles and attending introductory workshops. In the questioning stage, professionals raise questions about why assessment is necessary and how it changes our work. Resistance entails pushing back against expectations of incorporating assessment into daily work and is evidenced by such arguments as "we can't measure what we do" or "our goals cannot be captured in writing." At the point of participation, practitioners conduct assessment but do so largely in order to comply with expectations. In the final stage, commitment, student affairs professionals recognize the value of assessment and actively strive to incorporate it into our daily work. Assessment, at this point, is valued and used to generate evidence to inform decisions.

In 2014, an informal questionnaire sent to the SAAL listserv (Elkins) asked practitioners to consider their student affairs divisions in light of Erwin's (1991) stages. Although limited by a low response rate (17%), the collective responses placed student affairs divisions generally between resistance and participation. When broken out by specific units, over half of the practitioners placed their senior student affairs officers in the commitment stage. Most practitioners, however, placed unit heads and staff in the participation stage. Well over a third of responders placed staff in areas such as residence life, career centers, and social justice education in the lower stages of questioning and resistance. Comments revealed that very few divisions collectively were at the commitment stage of assessment but that a great deal of variation resulted when looking at individual units within those divisions. Respondents identified factors such as time, lack of prioritization, lack of training and skills, and failure to analyze and use results as contributing to the placement of student affairs divisions and units in the resistance or participation stages. A number of respondents noted that individuals continue to collect satisfaction and usage data rather than information on student learning outcomes.

Bearing in mind the limitations of both sets of data, information gleaned from SAAL members (Elkins, 2014) and *Change* (Miller, 2012) suggest that higher education and student affairs generally comply with expectations to incorporate assessment into their work but continue to struggle to recognize the value of assessment or use it to make decisions. In fact, Miller's assertion that higher education has generally moved through the "stages of grief" into "something like acceptance" (p. 8) raises the question of why, nearly 30 years later, we are still struggling to reach acceptance of, or even simply participation with (Erwin, 1991), assessment as a central tenet of our work. Even the fact that we discuss assessment in the context of "stages of grief" suggests that we mourn the golden days of yore, before the existence of expectations that we take responsibility for student learning and development. These conclusions are corroborated by recent scholarship in the field that continues to argue *why* student affairs must assess student learning and development (Blimling, 2013; Bresciani et al., 2009b; Schuh, 2013; Schuh & Gansemer-Topf, 2010).

Evidence of Student Learning Outcomes. A review of the recent annual meetings of the leading student affairs professional organizations revealed limited numbers of conference presentations on the results of student learning assessments. Most assessment-related sessions focused on the importance of undertaking such efforts on campuses and, more likely, how to design and implement division- or unit-wide assessment plans. Although campus-specific learning outcomes results are not likely to capture the interest of program selection committees and, thus, are perhaps not as likely to be selected for inclusion in convention program slates, it remains worth noting that the emphases of assessment-related conference sessions continue to be *whether* and *how* to assess student learning.

The scholarship in higher education and student affairs over the past 5 years supports this assertion, suggesting that assessment of student outcomes remains an unfulfilled promise (Bresciani et al., 2009b; Ewell, 2009; Hersch & Keeling, 2013; Hutchings, Ewell, & Banta, 2012; Schuh, 2013). Schuh and Gansemer-Topf (2010) argued that student affairs assessment had moved away from tracking participation and student satisfaction to a greater focus on student learning. They maintained, however, that student affairs is often overlooked in learning outcomes assessment because academic affairs generally takes the helm when evaluating student learning. In addition, they noted that although researchers (Jankowski & Makela, 2010; Kuh & Ikenberry, 2009) could specify what assessments were being conducted on campuses, the results of those assessments were rarely available.

Miller (2012) suggested that the glacial pace of progress in assessing student learning outcomes stemmed from multiple issues, including fear that the results will make individual faculty or staff "look bad" as well as our "collective intellectual hubris" of being asked to demonstrate the effectiveness of our work (p. 4). She further speculated that higher education's failure to assess student learning outcomes resulted from continued arguments over whether to articulate learning goals, and, if so, what they should be. As a result, calls for assessment typically are met by institutions who begrudgingly administer surveys but who miss the point of the demands—that is, "too little learning" (Hersch & Keeling, 2013, p. 4).

To be certain, there are higher education institutions and student affairs divisions with clearly articulated learning goals for students and well-designed and implemented means for assessing student outcomes. The literature is replete with examples of institutions and student affairs divisions doing good work focused on student learning outcomes assessment (Banta & Palomba, 2014; Banta, Jones, & Black, 2009; Bresciani et al., 2009a, 2009b). The fact, however, that continued cries for student affairs to engage in the assessment of student learning pepper the literature and shape the offerings of professional conferences suggests that, for the majority of student affairs divisions and professionals, much work remains to be done.

What the Future Holds

Progress in student affairs assessment has been painstakingly slow and fraught with challenges for individual institutions (Blimling, 2013; Bresciani et al., 2009b). Well over a decade into the new century, exhortations for student affairs professionals to assess student learning outcomes continue to proliferate (Allen et al., 2013; Blimling, 2013; Bresciani et al., 2009b; Schuh, 2013; Schuh & Gansemer-Topf, 2010). We must ask why our progress has been limited and sluggish, and, as a result, why we continue to struggle to (a) make assessment a routine part of our daily work, (b) document and evaluate student learning, and (c) demonstrate the essential role student affairs plays in student success. Furthermore, we must ask—and honestly answer—what will motivate us to change. If nearly 30 years' worth of encouraging and cajoling from leading scholars in higher education, student affairs, and assessment has not motivated us to critically examine whether, what, and how student learning occurs through our work, what will?

I suspect for many of us change will come only after losing staff when their arenas of employment are deemed "nonessential" or losing entire student affairs units when we are unable to demonstrate their contribution to students' educational experiences (Blimling, 2013). To avoid Blimling's concern that student affairs will become "little more than a staff function dedicated to the management of buildings, programs, and services for students" (p. 8), we must re-envision our work. To do so, we must take the following simple, albeit not necessarily easy, steps.

Stop Abdicating Responsibility for Student Learning. Before we can take responsibility for assessment, we must take responsibility for student success and learning. For decades, professional student affairs organizations and scholars (e.g., ACPA, 1994; ACPA & NASPA, 2004; Blimling, Whitt, & Associates, 1999; Kuh, Kinzie, Schuh, & Whitt, 2005; Upcraft & Schuh, 1996) have implored us to assume responsibility for student learning and development. Despite these calls to focus on student learning, assessment workshops continue to be filled with student affairs professionals who claim that learning is the purview of the faculty, that program outcomes are impossible to measure, or that focusing on learning takes away from the services or programs students need. In fact, much of what students learn through cocurricular experiences—e.g., leadership skills, working in teams—represents exactly the type of learning employers want (Hart Research Associates, 2013). These areas of learning can be broken down further into explicit skills and abilities highlighted by institutional learning outcomes. For instance, leadership skills consist of critical thinking, oral communication, and even writing skills, each of which is noted in the Association of American Colleges and University's (AAC&U, 2008) learning outcomes. Furthermore, they are learned across the span of the undergraduate experience, not only in class (Hersch & Keeling, 2013). Student affairs divisions must claim student learning and examine the cocurriculum for it.

Build Relationships With Faculty. Long before student affairs professionals can collaborate with faculty to assess student learning (Blimling, 2013; Hersch & Keeling, 2013; Schuh & Gansemer-Topf, 2010), we must work to build relationships with them. We will not be successful in arguing how out-of-class experiences contribute to overall student learning if we attempt to do so while standing on our side of the proverbial junior high gymnasium. We must reach across the divide not with the purposes of getting faculty to collaborate or convincing them of the value of student affairs. Rather we must reach out with the intentions of getting to know them, learning about their interests, and seeing students and student learning from their perspectives. As we build relationships, opportunities to engage in conversations about student learning will emerge. If we acknowledge that student learning is complex, multidimensional, and occurring over contexts and time (Astin et al., 1992; Ewell, 2009; Hersch & Keeling, 2013), crafting seamless learning environments in which faculty and student affairs professionals assume responsibility for, and collaborate to foster, student learning is critical (Schroeder, 1999). We will continue to find those steps nearly impossible to take without first building relationships on our campuses.

Adopt a "Just Do It" Attitude Toward Assessment. For decades we have been *talking* about assessment—arguing about its pertinence to student affairs work; debating whether we exist to provide services and programs or to foster student learning; developing and discussing plans for assessing student needs, satisfaction, and eventually student learning; and lamenting the vast array of challenges that prevent us from fully engaging in the assessment of student learning outcomes. To an outside observer, it might appear as though we are attempting to avoid *doing* assessment work. Indeed, it is well past time to stop talking—discussing, debating, arguing, lamenting—and to start doing. Strategies have been developed and shared for addressing the challenges we face (e.g., lack of time, resources, and understanding of student development and learning theories) in assessing student learning (Blimling, 2013; Bresciani et al., 2009b; Schuh & Gansemer-Topf, 2010). We simply need to pick them up and use them.

Conclusion

The fact that we continue to have similar, if not the same, conversations about assessment, as Ewell (2009) noted, attests to the fact that it is neither easy nor simple. Certainly in student affairs, assessment of student learning is fraught with challenges, not the least of which are lack of time, lack of resources, and limited assessment knowledge and skills (Bresciani et al., 2009b). Ultimately, however, our limited commitment to assessment stems from a lack of willingness to claim responsibility for student learning and make its assessment a priority for our work. In so doing, we shirk our responsibility to be good stewards of both institutional and student resources. We risk being deemed unnecessary to the institutional mission, particularly in times of tight resources and greater demands for accountability (Blimling, 2013). Indeed, without demonstrated evidence of our contribution to student learning, we risk our very future. The time for student outcomes assessment has passed. We cannot afford another 30 years of limited progress. We can begin by claiming our responsibility for student learning, building relationships with faculty, and taking a "just do it" attitude toward assessment of student learning.

References

Allen, K. R., Elkins, B., Henning, G. W., Bayless, L. A., & Gordon, T. W. (2013). *Accreditation and the role of the student affairs professional.* Washington, DC: American College Personnel Association.

American College Personnel Association (ACPA). (1994). *The student learning imperative: Implications for student affairs.* Washington, DC: Author.

American College Personnel Association (ACPA). (2007). *ASK standards: Assessment skills and knowledge content standards for student affairs practitioners and scholars.* Washington, DC: Author.

American College Personnel Association (ACPA) & National Association of Student Personnel Administrators (NASPA). (2004). *Learning reconsidered: A campus-wide focus on the student experience.* Washington, DC: Author.

American College Personnel Association (ACPA) & National Association of Student Personnel Administrators (NASPA). (2009). *Professional competency areas for student affairs practitioners.* Washington, DC: Author.

Association of American Colleges and Universities (AAC&U). (2008). *College learning for the new global century: A report from the National Leadership Council for Liberal Education and America's Promise.* Washington, DC: Author.

Astin, A. W., Banta, T. W., Cross, K. P., El-Khawas, E., Ewell, P. T., Hutchings, P., ... & Wright, B. D. (1992). *Nine principles of good practice for assessing student learning.* Washington, DC: American Association for Higher Education, Assessment Forum.

Banta, T. W. (2002). *Building a scholarship of assessment.* San Francisco, CA: Jossey-Bass.

Banta, T. W. (2004). *Hallmarks of effective outcomes assessment.* San Francisco, CA: Jossey-Bass.

Banta, T. W., Jones, E. A., & Black, K. E. (2009). *Designing effective assessment: Principles and profiles of good practice.* San Francisco, CA: Jossey-Bass.

Banta, T. W., & Palomba, C. A. (2014). *Assessment essentials: Planning, implementing, and improving assessment in higher education* (2nd ed.). San Francisco, CA: Jossey-Bass.

Barham, J. D., Tschepikow, W. K., & Seagraves, B. (2013). Creating a culture of assessment. In D. M. Timm, J. D. Barham, K. McKinney, & A. R. Knerr (Eds.), *Assessment in practice: A companion guide to the ASK Standards* (pp. 73–85). Washington, DC: American College Personnel Association.

Barr, R. B., & Tagg, J. (1995). From teaching to learning: A new paradigm for undergraduate education. *Change, 27,* 12–25.

Blimling, G. S. (2013). Challenges of assessment in student affairs. In J. H. Schuh (Ed.), *New Directions for Student Services: No. 142. Selected contemporary assessment issues* (pp. 5–14). San Francisco, CA: Jossey-Bass.

Blimling, G. S., Whitt, E. J., & Associates. (1999). *Good practice in student affairs: Principles for fostering student learning.* San Francisco, CA: Jossey-Bass.

Bresciani, M. J., Moore Gardner, M., & Hickmott, J. (2009a). *New Directions for Student Services: No. 127. Case studies for implementing assessment in student affairs.* San Francisco, CA: Jossey-Bass.

Bresciani, M. J., Moore Gardner, M., & Hickmott, J. (2009b). *Demonstrating student success: A practical guide to outcomes-based assessment of learning and development in student affairs.* Sterling, VA: Stylus.

Elkins, B. (2014). *Student affairs assessment questionnaire.* Unpublished report, Cornell College, Mount Vernon, IA.

Elling, T., & Bentrim, E. (2013, June 28). *Who is coordinating assessment in student affairs divisions? A roundtable conversation.* Paper presented at the NASPA Assessment and Persistence Conference, Denver, CO.

Erwin, T. D. (1991). *Assessing student learning and development: A guide to the principles, goals and methods of determining college outcomes.* San Francisco, CA: Jossey-Bass.

Ewell, P. T. (2002). An emerging scholarship: A brief history of assessment. In T. W. Banta (Ed.), *Building a scholarship of assessment* (pp. 3–25). San Francisco, CA: Jossey-Bass.

Ewell, P. T. (2009, November). *Assessment, accountability, and improvement: Revisiting the tension* (NILOA Occasional Paper No. 1). Urbana, IL: University of Illinois and Indiana University, National Institute for Learning Outcomes Assessment.

Hart Research Associates. (2013). *It takes more than a major: Employer priorities for college learning and success.* Retrieved from https://www.aacu.org/sites/default/files/files/LEAP/2013_EmployerSurvey.pdf

Hersch, R. H., & Keeling, R. P. (2013, February). *Changing institutional culture to promote assessment of higher learning* (Occasional Paper No. 17). Urbana, IL: University of Illinois and Indiana University, National Institute for Learning Outcomes Assessment.

Hutchings, P., Ewell, P. T., & Banta, T. W. (2012). *AAHE principles of good practice: Aging nicely.* Urbana, IL: University of Illinois and Indiana University, National Institute for Learning Outcomes Assessment. Retrieved from http://www.learningoutcomeassessment.org/PrinciplesofAssessment.html

Jankowski, N., & Makela, J. P. (2010). *Exploring the landscape: What institutional websites reveal about student learning outcomes activities.* Urbana, IL: University of Illinois and Indiana University, National Institute for Learning Outcomes Assessment.

Kübler-Ross, E. (1997). *On death and dying.* New York, NY: Scribner.

Kuh, G. D., & Ikenberry, S. (2009). *More than you think, less than we need: Learning outcomes assessment in American higher education.* Urbana, IL: University of Illinois and Indiana University, National Institute for Learning Outcomes Assessment.

Kuh, G. D., Kinzie, J., Schuh, J. H., & Whitt, E. J. (2005). *Student success in college: Creating conditions that matter.* San Francisco, CA: Jossey-Bass.

Livingston, C. H., & Zerulik, J. D. (2013). The role of the assessment coordinator in a division of student affairs. In J. H. Schuh (Ed.), *New Directions for Student Services: No. 142. Selected contemporary assessment issues* (pp. 15–24). San Francisco, CA: Jossey-Bass.

Malaney, G. D. (1997, May). *The structure and function of student affairs research offices: A national study.* Paper presented at the annual meeting of the Association for Institutional Research, Orlando, FL.

Miller, M. (2012). *From denial to acceptance: The stages of assessment* (NILOA Occasional Paper No. 13). Urbana, IL: University of Illinois and Indiana University, National Institute for Learning Outcomes Assessment.

National Governors' Association. (1986). *Time for results: The governors' 1991 report on education.* Washington, DC: Author.

National Institute for Education. (1984). *Involvement in learning: Realizing the potential of American Higher Education. Final report of the Study Group on the Conditions of Excellence in American Higher Education.* Washington, DC: Author.

Palomba, C. A., & Banta, T. W. (1999). *Assessment essentials: Planning, implementing, and improving assessment in higher education.* San Francisco, CA: Jossey-Bass.

Schroeder, C. C. (1999). Forging educational partnerships that advance student learning. In G. S. Blimling, E. J. Whitt, & Associates (Eds.), *Good practice in student affairs: Principles to foster student learning* (pp. 133–156). San Francisco, CA: Jossey-Bass.

Schuh, J. H. (2013). Developing a culture of assessment in student affairs. In J. H. Schuh (Ed.), *New Directions for Student Services: No. 142. Selected contemporary assessment issues* (pp. 89–98). San Francisco, CA: Jossey-Bass.

Schuh, J. H., & Gansemer-Topf, A. (2010, December). *The role of student affairs in student learning assessment* (NILOA Occasional Paper No. 7). Urbana, IL: University of Illinois and Indiana University, National Institute for Learning Outcomes Assessment.

Schuh, J. H., & Upcraft, M. L. (2001). *Assessment practice in student affairs: An applications manual.* San Francisco, CA: Jossey-Bass.

Suskie, L. (2009). *Assessing student learning* (2nd ed.). San Francisco, CA: Jossey-Bass.

Swing, R. L., & Coogan, C. S. (2010, May). *Valuing assessment: Cost-benefit considerations* (NILOA Occasional Paper No. 5). Urbana, IL: University of Illinois and Indiana University, National Institute for Learning Outcomes Assessment.

Upcraft, M. L., & Schuh, J. H. (1996). *Assessment in student affairs: A guide for practitioners.* San Francisco, CA: Jossey-Bass.

BECKI ELKINS *is registrar and director of institutional research and assessment at Cornell College.*

5

This chapter describes the student affairs profession in the digital age. The authors explore new challenges educators and professionals face as new areas are added and expanded, how social networks and digital technology tools continue to evolve, and what skills are needed to engage with students in person and online.

The Digital Age of Student Affairs

Edmund T. Cabellon, Reynol Junco

The growth and ubiquity of digital and social technology have transformed our society. Forty-five million Americans use mobile phones as their primary Internet device (Duggan & Smith, 2013a) and nearly 26% of all college students are enrolled in some form of online education (Ginder & Stearns, 2014). Further, nearly 73% of adults with Internet access use a social networking site, particularly Facebook and/or Twitter (Duggan & Smith, 2013b). Coupled with this technological revolution is the evolution of student affairs on college and university campuses. The function of student affairs units in higher education continues to evolve and expand: since 2000, many additional operational functions have been added under the auspices of student affairs units to support the growing complexity of needs associated with the contemporary student (McClellan & Stringer, 2009). For example, the addition of professional roles in key areas such as first-year programs, disability resources, marketing, technology, legal counsel, financial aid, admissions, and facility operations has decentralized broad university functions and led to more oversight and direction from student affairs practitioners. Additionally, support services for underrepresented populations such as gay, lesbian, bisexual, transgendered, and allied (GLBTA) students, commuters, and veterans have increased. Themed housing options such as living–learning communities have also seen an uptick in popularity, with the expressed goal of promoting student engagement and integration into the academic and social fabric of the institution. Although student affairs practitioners recognize the growth and specialization of practice within the profession, they also are responding to the implications and intricacies of digital and social technology in students' lives. These potentially competing priorities demand a nimble and innovative response, based on new definitions of the functions of student affairs in the digital age and new

New Directions for Student Services, no. 151, Fall 2015 © 2015 Wiley Periodicals, Inc.
Published online in Wiley Online Library (wileyonlinelibrary.com) • DOI: 10.1002/ss.20137

understanding of the promising possibilities of engagement with students through digital and social technologies.

This chapter provides a foundation and framework for student affairs practitioners regarding the use of digital and social technologies in their work with students and in serving students effectively. The chapter explores the growth of student affairs functions, how new communication and digital paradigms have expanded the way we engage with and understand students, and what skills and insight student affairs practitioners need to develop in order to foster an effective and engaged digital mind-set.

The Growth of Student Affairs Functions

Through much of the history of student affairs, practitioners have focused their attention on educating the whole student. More recently, student affairs work also has required balancing internal and external needs and demands, including expanding federal, state, and local regulations (Dungy & Gordon, 2011). Their roles in the academy have blended as practitioners, educators, and counselors, requiring a range of competencies including multiculturalism, student development, assessment, legal issues, and budget and finance (Herdlein, Riefler, & Mrowka, 2013).

Dungy and Gordon (2011) noted the development of the student affairs profession from its early beginnings of *in loco parentis* and the impact of high profile student activism to shifts in student demographics and new pathways to a degree in higher education. Manning, Kinzie, and Schuh (2014) expanded the literature regarding various student affairs administrative models. These include traditional (extracurricular, cocurricular, functional silos, and student services) and innovative (student-driven, academic-student affairs collaboration, academic-driven) approaches reflecting how various institutions organized student affairs functions. Further, the nomenclature for student affairs varies among public and private institutions alike. Some colleges refer to student affairs as "student life," "student services," or "student development." Given the disparity of its various models and classifications, one can see how challenging it can be to those outside of the student affairs profession to understand its purpose.

As institutions and students diversify, student affairs practitioners have adapted to meet these needs through the expansion of programs and services (McClellan & Stringer, 2009). Since the turn of the century, institutions have formed efforts and offices focused on first-year programs, recreational sports, community standards (conduct), and mental health (Tull & Kuk, 2013). Moreover, universities have also increased the creation of centers that support disenfranchised groups of students, such as GLBTA, multicultural, women, and veterans. As student affairs functions have expanded, so have new types of student affairs practitioners, particularly in enrollment, financial aid, technology, fundraising, communications, and assessment.

Conversely, there is speculation that the growth in student affairs–related areas has contributed to the rise in overall university tuition and fees, which have garnered scrutiny in a time where higher education costs have skyrocketed (Selingo, 2013). As student loan debt reaches historic levels of nearly $1 trillion (Desilver, 2014), students and families expect more from their college education and related experiences (Fry & Caumont, 2014). This puts increasing pressure on student affairs areas to demonstrate their value through cocurricular learning outcomes, assessment data, and skills built through engagement.

As higher education continues to evolve in the 21st century, so must the student affairs profession (Kuk, 2012). As the various pathways to a college education and degrees grow with additions of online and hybrid degree offerings, how has the field of student affairs diversified its pathways to cocurricular engagement? Certainly, electronic portfolios, cocurricular transcripts, and social media communication are examples that skim the surface of possibilities. However, the digital age is more than the adoption and integration of technology and communication tools. It requires those seeking to engage college students to develop the mind-set, fluency, and skills necessary to add value and relevance to the contemporary college experience.

University budgets will continue to decrease as state and federal dollars continue to flow in other areas (Manning et al., 2014). The cost of a college education has outpaced inflation since the early 1980s (U.S. Bureau of Labor Statistics, 2010). The increased cost of attendance along with the rise of for-profit institutions has fueled the calls for accountability. What, if anything, are student affairs professionals doing to enhance the student experience? And given research on social media (see Junco, 2014), how are student affairs professionals leveraging new technologies to support student engagement and learning? Student affairs professionals must use digital and social technologies to engage students in new ways, market the value of the university's academic and cocurricular activities, and teach students how to leverage these tools to find and sustain work in the 21st century. Only then will student affairs thrive in the digital age and actualize the next evolution of professional practice. In a time where technological advances and their impact are ubiquitous on college campuses, the lack of fluency around digital and social technology is significant. Student affairs professionals are ill equipped to *meet students where they are* on social media, relegating these sites to minor roles in their own professional competency portfolios, which in turn leaves them with a lack of understanding of the full experience of our students.

Student Affairs 2.0

Digital and social technologies have the power to reimagine the student experience. Consider the growing pressures on student affairs professionals around expanding enrollment, the changing student demographic, and the expectations around retention and persistence to graduation (Kuk, 2012). The meaningful use of digital and social technologies heightens the complexities of these expectations as professionals continue to explore ways to integrate them into their work (Shirky, 2009). Among these include increasing engagement efforts in and out of the classroom through expanding communication paradigms in social networks, psychosocial implications of online identity development, and growing legal implications for online behaviors.

Whereas historically much of student engagement research focuses on traditional face-to-face interaction, newer research shares an expanded perspective of engaging students online through social networks, particularly Twitter. Junco, Heiberger, and Loken (2011) noted improved grades and increased levels of traditional measures of engagement among students who used Twitter compared to their counterparts who did not. This study highlighted how Twitter could be leveraged to support students' academic engagement, psychosocial development, and Chickering and Gamson's (1987) seven principles for good practice in undergraduate education. Additionally, Junco and others (2011) found that the deliberate use of Twitter also led to a culture of engagement that deepened interpersonal connection between students. Similarly, these findings are consistent with the teaching recommendations provided by Dunlap and Lowenthal (2009), who used Twitter as an additional social tool to supplement instruction and found that it can encourage real-time interactions, thus enhancing one's social presence (Burke, Marlow, & Lento, 2010).

Twitter has the potential to increase overall academic and social integration through online learning communities (Tinto, 1997) for networking and relationship building. For example, Twitter was used as a tool for extending the engagement of large lecture hall classrooms into smaller communities (Elavsky, Mislan, & Elavsky, 2011). In this study, participation rates were high, with 80% of the 300 students in their class actively engaged on Twitter, used mostly for class discussions and expanded dialogue. Elavsky and others (2011) discovered, "The Twitter stream discourse deepened and extended the class potential for engagement with the course themes in novel ways defied standard interpretation" (p. 225). Additionally, those who may have been less inclined to speak up in a large lecture course felt more comfortable with Twitter, which enabled greater class discussions.

As higher education expands online learning offerings, Twitter use in online classes can mimic the dynamics of in-person discussions. Revere and Kovach (2011) explored the effectiveness of online course design and student engagement, and found that Twitter built a strong learner-centered environment and made coursework more vibrant. The researchers noted enhanced student engagement as well as higher levels of learning through extended class discussions. Dunlap and Lowenthal (2009) also explored using Twitter in the online class environment in place of traditional learning management systems. The researchers' goal was to enhance social presence, aimed at increasing one's cognitive abilities to process and participate in online classes. Ironically, an indirect benefit of academically integrating Twitter was the increase in the faculty's own teaching presence increasing through better course management and meaningful student contact. Certainly, instructors who effectively incorporate Twitter as a learning tool in their online or hybrid courses could reasonably expect to achieve enhanced student engagement as well as higher levels of learning (Revere & Kovach, 2011). When framed properly, using Twitter in the classroom may provide student affairs professionals the key to meaningfully engage students in online environments. At the very least, use of a social technology such as Twitter helps student affairs professionals connect with students in a way that leverages a student-preferred method of communication in order to make the interpersonal connections necessary to engage students in the ways necessary to support academic success.

As more student affairs professionals engage with students in digital social spaces, how should traditional methods be considered? Initially, Junco (2014) highlights the important difference between adult and youth normative perspectives when expanding one's understanding of social networks. Generally, an *adult normative* perspective reflects an adult viewpoint, marked by a prescriptive approach, highlighted by negative beliefs, where the sole source of information is from themselves. Those who engage in the *adult normative* perspective often believe popular media's negative portrayals of youth technology use. Conversely, a *youth normative* perspective reflects a youth-centered viewpoint, marked by an inquisitive approach, highlighted by balanced beliefs, where the primary source of information is from youth themselves. Consider the number of adult normative messages college students receive around the use of social networks by the time they attend college—they have been repeatedly told that a normal part of their existence is wrong. For example, boyd (2014) highlights the struggles of teenagers who are criticized for socializing through their mobile devices and social networks yet are never taught to expand the use of technology outside of social constructs. Additionally, the number of administrative school policies prohibiting mobile and social technologies in school, along with mainstream media messages around its negative impact (Junco, 2014), prevent any level of meaningful adoption on either perspective. Indeed, understanding the impact of both of these perspectives and how student affairs professionals expand their understanding into a *youth normative* perspective is an important step to understanding and implementation.

Next, student affairs professionals must consider how online identity development expands and complements traditional student development theory. Higher education practitioners and student development or related graduate programs must explore ways in which digital and social technologies have shifted related and connected scholarship. Although this area of research is unchartered and vast, given the depth and breadth of current literature on student development, the importance of such exploration is noteworthy. Junco (2014) notes:

> The identity development models reviewed thus far focus exclusively on identity development in the offline world—the expression of and interaction within a community that leads to changes and movement along a developmental path. However, the emergence of online social spaces has allowed youth to explore their identities in ways not previously possible. (p. 105)

Additionally, student affairs practitioners must find ways to incorporate online identity development into programs and services. Some examples may include digital identity conversations at orientation and various leadership programs, student employment training, and professional competency building programs through career services. Junco (2014) also noted the importance of recognizing and teaching three levels of expressed online identification: "True Identity," "Pseudonymity," and "Anonymity" (p. 106). The more-obfuscated forms of identification allow students to explore their identities in ways not previously possible. Student affairs practitioners must give pause to reflect on how they may have engaged in digital and social communication before teaching their students about its values and consequences.

Furthermore, legal issues pertaining to digital and social technologies should be considered in all student affairs settings. Binder and Mansfield (2013) note important issues such as privacy law, intellectual property ownership, and mandatory reporting of anonymous speech, particularly around sexual violence. One way to address these concerns is to create a cross-divisional university committee composed of staff, faculty, and legal counsel to create guidance documents on digital and social technology use. Additionally, student affairs professionals should complement these guidance documents with proper training tools such as case law. For example, in *Tatro v. University of Minnesota*, the University of Minnesota and its Mortuary Science Program expelled Amanda Tatro based on comments posted to Facebook while off campus (Levine, 2013). Whereas Tatro claimed her comments were part of her First Amendment rights, the case matched decisions levied by the U.S. Supreme Court decisions in *Tinker v. Des Moines Independent County School District* and *Bethel School District No. 403 v. Fraser,* which assessed student's rights to free speech as applied in light of special characteristics of a school environment. In other words, *Tinker* allowed school officials to restrict student speech when it is reasonably likely to cause a material and substantial disruption of school activities. In the *Tatro* case, the Minnesota Supreme Court found that the right to freedom of speech did not protect Tatro, because her Facebook posts violated the university's academic guidelines.

The contemporary student requires an intentional level of digital and social technology education and training in order to prepare them appropriately for citizenship in the digital age. Whether the focus is on engaging students in and out of the classroom, gaining an expanded view of identity through social networks, or developing a more holistic view on legal issues related to the use of digital communication tools, student affairs professionals must assume a leadership role in these initiatives (Tull & Kuk, 2013). Although the barriers to this shift in curricula and cocurricular endeavors remain visible, student affairs staff should consider strategic ways in which they can act swiftly to discover better ways to address student digital and technological skills in and outside the academic setting.

Student Affairs Pixelation

In the world of digital photography, pixelated images look blurry, often because the image has been enlarged without simultaneously increasing the resolution. This creates a low-quality image that sometimes makes it difficult to identify the subject. Similarly, the field of student affairs appears pixelated due to its rapid growth in response to the diverse needs of today's college students (Dungy & Gordon, 2011) and an increased focus on student success (Bowen, 2013). How can the student affairs profession increase its resolution? First, student affairs professionals must identify how its functions will be defined in online or hybrid environments (Shea & Blakely, 2002). Certainly, with the rise of project based degrees and immersive curriculum focused on the gamification of learning, student affairs practitioners can no longer ignore technology's impact in the academy (Selingo, 2013). Second, student affairs professionals must clearly articulate what types of digital and social technology skills are needed to engage this generation of students. This is important due to the work professional organizations such as the National Association of Student Personnel Administrators (NASPA) and the American College Personnel Association (ACPA) are undertaking to update guidance documents on professional competencies. Third, student affairs professionals should explore ways to use data around digital and social technology use to help inform practice and share stories around the impact of their work. Indeed, the combination may unlock the clearest picture of the student affairs profession we have.

A common question posed among student affairs professionals around the use of digital and social technologies is how student affairs functions will manifest in online environments. However, this question moves beyond the literature that discusses social networks, technology's psychosocial impacts, and student engagement. Of course, this question seeks to understand how to connect, engage, and support those students who do not physically come to campus. Dare, Zapata, and Thomas (2005) noted seven recommendations for student affairs professionals:

1. Understand the administration of distance learning programs.
2. Understand the vocabulary of distance learning.

3. Understand the funding of distance learning programs.
4. Be prepared to advocate for the role of student affairs in distance learn-ing and to educate others about the mission, function, and objectives in student affairs units.
5. Advocate for equal services for students who take courses online and on campus.
6. Develop programs to meet the unique needs of online students.
7. Establish positions with duties focused entirely on the needs of online students. (as cited in Crawley & LeGore, 2009, p. 297)

Although these recommendations provide a starting point for impor-tant conversation, it is equally important to recognize the convenience of online courses being the driving force behind those enrolled (Crawley & LeGore, 2009). Patience and understanding of this unchartered territory is required, as this may negate some of student affairs' intentional efforts to connect with online students.

In order for student affairs professionals to achieve some or all of these recommendations, they must first understand how to implement change in their institution's organizational structure (Bess & Dee, 2012). Certainly, good practices to achieve these important changes exist, and vary with size and focus of the institution. That is to say that what may work at a small pri-vate college would not work at a large research university. Still, by working with key staff across university departments and divisions, particularly in academic affairs, student affairs professionals have a greater chance in build-ing and sustaining movement toward a focus around engaging students in online environments. Second, the use of external consultants through the program review process may serve as change agents by adding expertise into existing conversation (Crawley & LeGore, 2009). Third, consulting and collaborating with similar institutions that are actively engaging students online provides another level of evidence that may lay the groundwork for increased staffing and resources around online student engagement efforts. Effective resource allocation is reliant on student affairs professionals pur-suing evidence indicating online student engagement efforts are directly related to student retention.

As the student affairs profession continues to evolve in the digital age, so do the depth and breadth of its competencies (Council for the Ad-vancement of Standards in Higher Education [CAS], 2012; National As-sociation of Student Personnel Administrators [NASPA], 2010). It is stan-dard for many student affairs professional organizations to have specific competencies for each of their functional areas, such as the Association of College Unions International (ACUI), the Association of College and University Housing Officers International, and the National Association for Campus Activities. CAS (2012) highlights 38 functional areas in higher ed-ucation, particularly in student affairs, documenting area standards, and specific learning outcomes. Additionally, NASPA (2010), along with ACPA, share one guiding document for student affairs professionals around 10 professional competencies: Advising and Helping; Assessment, Evaluation, and Research; Equity, Diversity, and Inclusion; Ethical Professional Practice; History, Philosophy, and Values; Human and Organizational Resources; Law, Policy, and Governance; Leadership; Personal Foundations; and Student Learning and Development. Each competency is broken into three competency area levels (beginner, intermediate, and advanced) to allow for learning on a continuum. Surprisingly, even with these and other higher education standards, there still lacks a widely accepted higher education or student affairs competency in digital and social technology (Herdlein et al., 2013). The only association that has a competency focused on technology is ACUI, which defines this competency as the ability to understand the overall intent of digital tools and to choose from appropriate tools, equipment, and procedures for service delivery and problem solving.

Currently, technology is listed as a competency "area thread," along with sustainability and globalism (NASPA, 2010). These threads are considered as essential elements *as a part of* each competency area, rather than existing as their own separate competencies. In the digital age, student affairs professionals require clearer guidance in the absence of a national professional standard for the use of technology. The establishment of this standard may provide a matching framework for faculty to intentionally include digital technologies in their pedagogy. In its absence, faculty and staff continue to explore the merits of newer technology tools while students fail to gain valuable knowledge and skills necessary for postgraduate life. Thus, how can student affairs professionals begin to establish an industry-accepted technology standard? Jenkins (2009) noted 11 work skills that people need to be active contributors in the digital age, with 6 being focused around digital and social technologies:

1. Appropriation: The ability to meaningfully sample and remix media content.
2. Distributed cognition: The ability to interact meaningfully with tools that expand mental capacities.
3. Collective intelligence: The ability to pool knowledge and compare notes with others towards a common goal.
4. Judgment: The ability to evaluate the reliability and credibility of different information sources.
5. Transmedia Navigation: The ability to follow the flow of stories and information across multiple modalities.
6. Networking: The ability to search for, synthesize, and disseminate information. (p. 4)

Recognition of technology competencies would address the knowledge, skills, and mind-set around digital and social tools that provide important data. These data provide synthesized information and workflow efficiency to increase student engagement opportunities. Consider how each of the skills could begin translating this new competency. Transmedia Navigation, Judgment, and Collective Intelligence reflect the need to sift through the enormous amount of available data via the Internet and make meaning of it. Networking and Appropriation reflect the need to understand, synthesize, and present data in a way diverse audiences can relate and respond to. Distributed Cognition reflects the need to use tools that encourage critical thinking ensuring that the highest quality dialogue will take place. As NASPA and ACPA update student affairs competencies for 2015 and beyond, the hope is that technology emerges as a new competency for the profession.

As student affairs practitioners continue to integrate technology into their work, opportunities to use big data may help inform modern student affairs practice. For instance, large data sets may provide the foundation and infrastructure to share stories about the impact of student affairs in a digital age. Certainly, if data-driven evidence leads student affairs efforts (McClellan & Stringer, 2009), the emergence of big data use in higher education should become an important imperative. Picciano (2012) defines big data as information or database systems used as a main storage facility capable of storing large quantities of data longitudinally, down to very specific transactions. Applicable examples in higher education infrastructure include data in student information systems (for example, Banner), data stored through the use of student identification cards (e.g., checking in at the residence halls, library, recreational facility, or college events), and data from learning management systems (for example, Blackboard, Moodle). Additionally, website and application data provide information on frequency and use of various digital technology services available to the university community. Furthermore, social networks and mobile devices provide self-reported, location-based, and sentiment-filled data that give institutions an innovative view on the student experience. Big data can be analyzed in order to equip professionals with usable information to catalyze data-driven decisions; however, the data only *inform* those influencing decision making and should not be taken out of big picture context.

Harnessing the power of big data in student affairs is a complicated process, requiring political support across the institution (Johnson, Adams-Becker, Estrada, & Freeman, 2014). Cross-divisional partnerships are required, particularly within faculty leadership, in order to ensure diverse data points are represented. This is achieved, in part, through building a climate of trust around the process and the data and allowing open access to created dashboards. Indeed, recruitment, retention, research, and fundraising efforts have the potential to be positively impacted by these efforts. In support, Wishon and Rome (2012) noted that the initial creation of an enterprise data warehouse provides the necessary infrastructure needed to create reporting and analytic capability. Only then could the creation of data dashboards make it easier to access and consume information and give nontechnical users the ability to get answers for the questions they are asking. For instance, such a dashboard could identify the types of students who struggle in first-year science courses in order to plan appropriate interventions. Ultimately, big data have the ability to influence funding decisions in a time when financial and staffing resources continue to decrease (Manning et al., 2014).

In student affairs, decisions based on big data analytics have the potential to elucidate and improve upon the diverse types of student affairs work. Data warehouses such as "Degree Works" provide information about degree audits in a user-friendly format, providing timely information to academic advisors and students, focused on increasing retention and graduation rates. Cocurricular transcripts and electronic portfolios allow students to share how they have actualized classroom knowledge in ways that demonstrate marketable skills. Data represented through visual information graphics with complimentary, interactive websites provide salient information while measuring which data sets were engaged with most often. In fact, most website data are rich with information around frequency, time spent on the website, and how people were referred to your website (for example, from social networks, search engine, main university site). Also, social network data are often visually represented through heat maps, where bursts of colors represent high quantities of activity and through stories, constructed by combining single social network posts into one threaded web page. Finally, with the rapid growth of wearable and health-related mobile technologies, innovative applications to education may already be in production. When you combine digital data with the learning outcomes and program evaluation data, student affairs professionals have the potential to share powerful stories for prospective and current students, alumni, parents, and community.

Conclusion

The digital age of student affairs is rich with opportunities to enhance the student experience, both in person and online. As digital and social technologies evolve, educators have the opportunity to unlock new, innovative ways to engage the contemporary student and the university community. Of course, legal issues should be considered through well-developed guidance documents that support both faculty and administration's efforts and appropriately address concerns. However, opportunities to use digital information may provide university leaders the ability to make more informed decisions and provide timely initiatives to support student success. As more functional areas are added to the student affairs infrastructure, developing technological fluency provides important evidence toward student success and engagement. Seeking key supporters at one's institution and identifying good technology practices at peer institutions are the first steps in discovering the potential of social and digital technology.

References

Bess, J. L., & Dee, J. R. (2012). *Understanding college and university organization: Theories for effective policy and practice* (Vol. 2). Sterling, VA: Stylus.

Binder, P., & Mansfield, N. R. (2013). Social networks and workplace risk: Classroom scenarios from U.S. and EU perspective. *Journal of Legal Studies, 30*(1), 1–44.

Bowen, W. G. (2013). *Higher education in the digital age.* Princeton, NJ: Princeton University Press.

boyd, d. (2014). *It's complicated: The social lives of networked teens.* New Haven, CT: Yale University Press.

Burke, M., Marlow, C., & Lento, T. (2010, April). *Social networking activity and social well-being.* Paper presented at the CHI 2010 Proceedings of the SIGCHI Conference on Human Factors in Computing Systems, Atlanta, GA. Retrieved from http://dl.acm.org/citation.cfm?id=1753613

Chickering, A. W., & Gamson, Z. F. (1987). Seven principles for good practice. *American Association of Higher Education Bulletin, 39*, 3–7.

Council for the Advancement of Standards in Higher Education (CAS). (2012). *CAS professional standards for higher education* (8th ed.). Washington, DC: Author.

Crawley, A., & LeGore, C. (2009). Supporting online students. In G. S. McClellan & J. Stringer (Eds.), *The handbook of student affairs administration* (pp. 288–308). San Francisco, CA: Jossey-Bass.

Dare, L. A., Zapata, L. P., & Thomas, A. G. (2005). Assessing the needs of distance learners: A student affairs perspective. In K. Kruger (Ed.), *Technology in student affairs: Supporting student learning and services* (pp. 39–54). San Francisco, CA: Jossey-Bass.

Desilver, D. (2014, May 15). *By many measures, more borrowers struggling with student-loan payments.* Pew Research Center. Retrieved from http://www.pewresearch.org/fact-tank/2014/05/15/by-many-measures-more-borrowers-struggling-with-student-loan-payments/

Duggan, M., & Smith, A. (2013a, September 16). *Cell internet use 2013.* Pew Research Center. Retrieved from http://www.pewinternet.org/2013/09/16/cell-internet-use-2013/

Duggan, M., & Smith, A. (2013b, December 30). *Social media update 2013.* Pew Research Center. Retrieved from http://www.pewinternet.org/2013/12/30/social-media-update-2013/

Dungy, G., & Gordon, S. A. (2011). The development of student affairs. In J. H. Schuh, S. R. Jones, & S. R. Harper (Eds.), *Student services: A handbook for the profession* (5th ed., pp. 61–80). San Francisco, CA: Jossey-Bass.

Dunlap, J. C., & Lowenthal, P. R. (2009). Tweeting the night away: Using Twitter to enhance social presence. *Journal of Information Systems Education, 20*(2), 129–135.

Elavsky, C. M., Mislan, C., & Elavsky, S. (2011). When talking less is more: Exploring outcomes of Twitter usage in the large-lecture hall. *Learning, Media and Technology, 36*(3), 215–233.

Fry, R., & Caumont, A. (2014, May 14). *5 key findings about student debt.* Pew Research Center. Retrieved from http://www.pewresearch.org/fact-tank/2014/05/14/5-key-findings-about-student-debt/

Ginder, S., & Stearns, C. (2014, June 2). *Enrollment in distance education course, by state: Fall 2012.* Washington, DC: U.S. Department of Education, National Center for Education Statistics. Retrieved from http://nces.ed.gov/pubs2014/2014023.pdf

Herdlein, R., Riefler, L., & Mrowka, K. (2013). An integrative literature review of student affairs competencies: A meta-analysis. *Journal of Student Affairs Research and Practice, 50*(3), 250–269.

Jenkins, H. (2009). *Confronting the challenges of participatory culture: Media education for the 21st century.* Cambridge, MA: The MIT Press.

Johnson, L., Adams-Becker, S., Estrada, V., & Freeman, A. (2014). *NMC horizon report: 2014 higher education edition*. Austin, TX: New Media Consortium.

Junco, R. (2014). *Engaging students through social media: Evidence-based practices for use in student affairs*. San Francisco, CA: Jossey-Bass.

Junco, R., Heiberger, G., & Loken, E. (2011). The effect of Twitter on college student engagement and grades. *Journal of Computer Assisted Learning, 27*(2), 119–132.

Kuk, L. (2012). The changing nature of student affairs. In A. Tull & L. Kuk (Eds.), *New realities in the management of student affairs* (pp. 3–12). Sterling, VA: Stylus.

Levine, R. (2013). *Tatro v. University of Minnesota* (Case Brief). American Civil Liberties Union of Minnesota. Retrieved from http://www.aclu-mn.org/legal/casedocket /tatrovuniversityofminnesot/

Manning, K., Kinzie, J., & Schuh, J. H. (2014). *One size does not fit all: Traditional and innovative models of student affairs practice*. New York, NY: Routledge.

McClellan, G. S., & Stringer, J. (2009). *The handbook of student affairs administration*. San Francisco, CA: Jossey-Bass.

National Association of Student Personnel Administrators (NASPA). (2010). *Professional competency areas of student affairs practitioners*. Washington, DC: Author.

Picciano, A. G. (2012). The evolution of big data and learning analytics in American higher education. *Journal of Asynchronous Learning Networks, 16*(3), 9–20.

Revere, L., & Kovach, J. V. (2011). Online technologies for engaged learning. *Quarterly Review of Distance Education, 12*(2), 113–124.

Selingo, J. J. (2013). *College unbound: The future of higher education and what it means for students*. New York, NY: Houghton Mifflin.

Shea, P., & Blakely, B. (2002). Designing web-based student services—Collaboration style. In D. Burnett & D. Oblinger (Eds.), *Innovation in student services: Planning for models blending high touch/high tech* (pp. 161–175). Ann Arbor, MI: Society for College and University Planning.

Shirky, C. (2009). *Here comes everybody: The power of organizing without organizations*. New York, NY: Penguin.

Tinto, V. (1997). Classrooms as communities: Exploring the educational character of student persistence. *Journal of Higher Education, 68*(6), 599–623.

Tull, A., & Kuk, L. (2013). *New realities in the management of student affairs*. Sterling, VA: Stylus.

U.S. Bureau of Labor Statistics. (2010). *Back to college*. Retrieved from http://www.bls .gov/spotlight/2010/college/

Wishon, G. D., & Rome, J. (2012, August 13). Enabling a data-driven university. *EDUCAUSE Review*. Retrieved from http://www.educause.edu/ero/article/enabling -data-driven-university

EDMUND T. CABELLON *is assistant to the vice president of student affairs at Bridgewater State University and a doctoral candidate in educational leadership at Johnson and Wales University. He is also the co-chair of ACPA's Presidential Task Force on Digital Technology.*

REYNOL JUNCO *is an associate professor of education and human computer interaction at Iowa State University and a faculty associate at the Berkman Center for Internet and Society at Harvard University.*

6

This chapter traces the recent history of student affairs finance and offers suggestions for dealing with the financial challenges of the future.

Contemporary Challenges in Student Affairs Budgeting and Finance

Ann M. Gansemer-Topf, Peter D. Englin

In the 2003 publication *Contemporary Financial Issues in Student Affairs*, Schuh (2003) described the nature of the financial environment of colleges and universities as "challenging" and speculated that it was "unlikely to change in the foreseeable future" (p. 14). This speculation has proven to be accurate: state governmental support for public institutions has continued to erode, most institutions have increased their reliance on tuition as a revenue source, and the public is demanding more transparency and accountability from their higher education institutions. In addition, the past 10 years have included a significant economic recession, changes in student demographics, alterations of student loan and health care policies, and the proliferation of technology and social media that have resulted in an almost paradigmatic shift in how we communicate. These changes have affected the financial landscape of higher education and, unsurprisingly, have influenced the budgeting and finances of student affairs.

This chapter discusses current issues facing student affairs finances. Because student affairs is influenced by the broader institutional context, this chapter begins with an overview of trends in the revenues and expenditure patterns for higher education institutions. Next, most commonly used budget models are defined and factors affecting these models are identified. After this broader context is described, the discussion is narrowed to focus on the financial environment of student affairs. Changes in the past decade are described and a list of contemporary issues related to student affairs budget and finances is identified.

Revenues and Expenditures

Each year institutions that participate in federal student financial aid programs are required to complete a set of surveys known as the Integrated

We would like to thank Nicole Prentice for her assistance with manuscript preparation.

New Directions for Student Services, no. 151, Fall 2015 © 2015 Wiley Periodicals, Inc.
Published online in Wiley Online Library (wileyonlinelibrary.com) • DOI: 10.1002/ss.20138

Postsecondary Education Data System (IPEDS). These surveys collect data on a variety of institutional activities; the finance survey specifically focuses on institutional expenditures and revenues. Institutions have a finite number of financial resources but have flexibility in how they may allocate their resources. The longitudinal data collected through IPEDS provide the ability to examine trends in institutional revenue and how institutions choose to spend these resources. The first four tables provide an overview of the trends of revenues and expenditures of public and private institutions. IPEDS finance surveys are different for public and private institutions so the National Center for Education Statistics (NCES) mirrors these differences in their reports on revenues and expenditures.

Revenues. For both private and public institutions, tuition and fees are accounting for a larger percentage of revenues (see Tables 6.1 and 6.2). For private institutions, revenues from tuition and fees increased 10% (from 28.7 to 38.9) with tuition and fees now accounting for almost 40% of an institution's revenues. The percentage of revenues from tuition and fees increased almost 5%. In 2003–2004, tuition and fees accounted for 15.8% of the revenues and state appropriations accounted for 27.7%. In 2011–2012, tuition and fees increased to 20.6% and state appropriations decreased to 21.8%. Put another way, in the past decade, institutions relied on state appropriations for almost one fourth of their revenues and this percentage almost doubled that from tuition. In 2011–2012, state appropriations accounted for a little more than one fifth of an institution's revenues and almost equaled the percentage of revenues coming from tuition.

Reliance on tuition and fees may be increasing but most institutional leaders are aware that this practice cannot be sustained. Many institutions are looking externally to such strategies as fundraising and corporate sponsorship as a way to generate revenue (Green, Jaschik, & Lederman, 2012). Institutions are also focusing more internally in the areas of enrollment management, specifically in retention efforts, with the assumption that tuition increases can be kept at a minimum if more students stay enrolled (Jaschik & Lederman, 2013).

The impact in the economic recession is also evident in Tables 6.1 and 6.2. The percentage of revenues from investment returns were negative for 2008–2009 with a 3.6% decrease for public institutions and a 93% decrease for private institutions. In 2008–2009, significant increases in federal appropriations, especially at private institutions, were most likely due to programs such as the State Fiscal Stabilization Fund. This program, which was a part of the American Recovery and Reinvestment Act of 2009, contributed an influx of one-time funds to institutions (U.S. Department of Education, 2009). For public institutions, state appropriations peaked before the economic recession in 2007 and have declined since. Higher education institutions, although often chided as ivory towers separate from the "real world," have been and will continue to be affected by a broader socioeconomic context.

Table 6.1. Percentage of Current Fund Revenues From Various Sources by Public Degree-Granting Institutions, 2003–2004 Through 2011–2012

	Percentage								
Source	2003–2004	2004–2005	2005–2006	2006–2007	2007–2008	2008–2009	2009–2010	2010–2011	2011–2012
Student tuition and fees	15.8	16.4	17.0	16.7	17.6	19.4	18.4	18.6	20.6
Federal appropriations, grants, and contracts	14.9	14.8	14.2	13.2	13.7	15.3	16.9	17.3	17.1
State appropriations, grants, and contracts	27.7	26.9	27.3	26.9	28.6	28.3	23.9	22.7	21.8
Local and private appropriations, grants, and contracts	6.7	6.5	6.5	6.4	6.7	7.4	6.5	6.3	6.5
Gifts	1.9	2.0	2.0	2.1	2.2	2.2	1.9	1.9	2.1
Investment income	3.2	4.1	3.9	5.8	1.9	-3.6	3.3	4.4	1.9
Independent operations	0.4	0.3	0.3	0.3	0.4	0.4	0.4	0.4	0.4
Sales and services	16.5	16.8	16.6	16.0	16.7	18.2	17.0	16.9	18.2
Other sources	12.9	12.4	12.3	12.7	12.1	12.5	11.6	11.5	11.4

Note: Adapted from NCES (2008a, 2013a).

Table 6.2. Percentage of Current Fund Revenues From Various Sources by Private Degree-Granting Institutions, 2003–2004 Through 2011–2012

Source	Percentage								
	2003–2004	2004–2005	2005–2006	2006–2007	2007–2008	2008–2009	2009–2010	2010–2011	2011–2012
Student tuition and fees	28.7	29.5	29.0	26.0	36.4	77.8	33.4	29.0	38.9
Federal appropriations, grants, and contracts	13.7	14.1	12.9	11.1	14.5	30.4	13.6	11.7	14.9
State and local appropriations, grants, and contracts	1.5	1.4	1.4	1.2	1.7	3.5	1.3	1.1	1.2
Private gifts, grants, and contracts	11.8	11.9	12.0	11.1	15.1	25.6	10.7	10.7	13.4
Investment return	23.0	21.7	23.3	30.7	4.6	−93.0	16.9	25.9	2.8
Educational activities	2.5	2.6	2.4	2.3	3.5	6.9	2.9	2.4	3.1
Auxiliary enterprises	7.7	7.7	7.6	6.7	9.3	19.6	8.4	7.1	9.6
Hospitals	7.2	7.4	7.6	6.9	9.6	21.4	9.8	8.5	11.5
Other	4.1	3.7	3.9	4.1	5.3	7.7	3.2	3.7	4.5

Note: Adapted from NCES (2013b).

Expenditures.   Although institutions have seen significant changes in their revenue streams, their expenditure patterns have been relatively consistent (see Tables 6.3 and 6.4). In the past decade, expenditures at public institutions have declined slightly in the areas of instruction, research, public service, institutional support, auxiliary enterprises, and other expenses. Expenditures on academic support, student services, and physical plant have remained relatively stable, and expenditures on scholarship and fellowships, hospitals, and interest have increased slightly (NCES, 2013c). At private institutions, expenditures on research, public services, auxiliary enterprises, net grant aid to students, and independent operations have decreased. Unlike their public institution counterparts, expenditures on instruction, academic support, and student services expenditures have increased (NCES, 2013d).

Although revenue streams have fluctuated, the decisions on where to spend money have remained remarkably stable. The limitation with these data, of course, is that it is not evident how institutions have chosen to spend their money. For example, public institutions may have been able to spend less on instruction by converting courses to online and creating larger sections of courses. Student services expenditures include activities related to admissions offices, so some private institutions may have devoted more funds in this areas as a way to increase enrollment. Despite the limitations of these data, viewing these trends can provide at least a general overview of the changes and consistencies in the revenues and expenditures of higher education institutions.

Student Services Expenditures by Carnegie Classification and Institutional Selectivity

Tables 6.1 and 6.2 provide insight into differences between public and private institutions, but institutions within these categories vary significantly. Carnegie Classification and institutional selectivity are two additional ways of investigating expenditures. For the purpose of this chapter we focus on student services expenditures and examine how the percentage and amount of student services expenditures have changed over time for institutions that differ in Carnegie Classification and institutional selectivity.

Carnegie Classification.   Tables 6.5 and 6.6 demonstrate these differences by Carnegie Classification. Data were collected using the IPEDS database. The 2010 Basic Carnegie Classification variable was used and institutions were then grouped into four classification types: Associate's, Baccalaureate, Master's, and Research. The years 2001–2002, 2005–2006, and 2011–2012 were used to provide a snapshot of expenditures over 10 years.

Baccalaureate institutions spend more money and dedicate a higher percentage of their resources to student services than do other institutions. Master's institutions dedicate a lower percentage of expenditures on student

Table 6.3. Percentage of Current Fund Expenditures of Public Degree-Granting Institutions, by Purpose, 2003–2004 Through 2011–2012

Purpose	Percentage								
	2003–2004	2004–2005	2005–2006	2006–2007	2007–2008	2008–2009	2009–2010	2010–2011	2011–2012
Instruction	27.7	27.7	27.8	28.1	27.5	27.5	27.1	26.8	26.5
Research	10.4	10.5	10.2	10.0	9.7	9.8	10.0	9.9	9.7
Public service	4.4	4.4	4.3	4.3	4.1	4.1	4.1	4.0	3.9
Academic support	6.6	6.6	6.8	6.8	6.9	6.9	6.7	6.5	6.6
Student services	4.6	4.7	4.7	4.8	4.7	4.7	4.7	4.6	4.6
Institutional support	8.2	8.1	8.2	8.4	8.5	8.5	8.1	8.1	7.9
Physical plant	6.2	6.3	6.7	6.6	6.5	6.5	6.4	6.4	6.3
Scholarships and fellowships	4.0	3.9	3.8	3.8	3.7	4.1	5.5	6.0	5.4
Depreciation	4.4	4.5	4.5	4.5	4.9	5.0	5.1	5.2	5.4
Auxiliary enterprises	7.7	7.7	7.6	7.8	7.5	7.5	7.3	7.3	7.3
Hospitals	9.0	9.3	9.1	9.3	9.2	9.5	9.5	9.4	10.1
Independent operations	0.4	0.3	0.3	0.3	0.4	0.4	0.4	0.4	0.4
Interest	1.3	1.2	1.5	1.6	1.7	1.1	1.8	1.9	2.0
Other	5.2	4.8	4.6	3.9	4.8	4.4	3.4	3.5	3.8

Note: Adapted from NCES (2008b, 2013c).

Table 6.4. Percentage of Current Fund Expenditures of Private Degree-Granting Institutions, by Purpose, 2003–2004 Through 2011–2012

Purpose	Percentage									
	2003–2004	2004–2005	2005–2006	2006–2007	2007–2008	2008–2009	2009–2010	2010–2011	2011–2012
Instruction	32.5	32.8	32.9	33.1	33.1	32.9	32.7	32.6	32.7
Research	11.5	11.6	11.3	11.0	10.8	10.8	11.1	11.4	10.9
Public service	1.9	1.8	1.7	1.6	1.6	1.6	1.4	1.5	1.5
Academic support	8.4	8.5	8.8	8.7	8.9	8.9	8.9	8.9	8.9
Student services	7.2	7.4	7.7	7.7	7.8	7.8	7.9	8.0	8.1
Institutional support	13.4	13.3	13.4	13.5	13.8	13.7	13.4	13.3	13.2
Auxiliary enterprises	10.1	9.9	10.1	10.0	10.0	9.7	9.6	9.5	9.4
Net grant aid to students	1.1	1.0	0.6	0.6	0.5	0.5	0.6	0.5	0.5
Hospitals	8.0	8.3	8.3	8.4	8.1	8.4	9.1	9.3	9.7
Independent operations	4.1	3.8	3.6	3.8	3.7	3.7	3.6	3.5	3.4
Other	1.9	1.5	1.7	1.6	1.7	2.0	1.8	1.5	1.8

Note: Adapted from NCES (2013d).

Table 6.5. Average Percentage Student Services Expenditures by Carnegie Classification

	Percentage		
Classification	2001–2002	2005–2006	2011–2012
Associate's	9.2	9.6	10.6
Baccalaureate	13.4	14.9	16.4
Master's	11.1	11.8	13.4
Research	5.8	5.9	6.8

services but outpace Research and Associate's. Associate's colleges spend the least amount per student but have the second lowest percentage dedicated to student services. Research institutions dedicate the lowest percentage of expenditures to student services but spend significantly more per student than Associate's colleges and almost the same amount per student as Master's colleges.

Institutional Selectivity. Institutional selectivity is the degree of admissions competitiveness. Selectivity is based on incoming students' average exam scores (for example, SAT/ACT), high school rank, high school grade point average, and the percentage of applicants who were accepted (Barron's Educational Series, 2009). Higher selectivity institutions have more financial resources and tend to have higher retention and graduation rates than less selective institutions (Bowen, Chingos, & McPherson, 2009; Gansemer-Topf & Schuh, 2006; Titus, 2006). *Barron's Profiles of American Colleges* (Barron's Educational Series, 2009) ranks institutions on a scale of "1" not competitive to "6" most competitive. Data from Barron's Educational Series (2009) were merged with IPEDS data to develop Tables 6.7 and 6.8.

Table 6.7 illustrates that for all institutions except the most competitive institutions, the percentage of expenditures increased from 2001–2002 to 2011–2012, and the last 5 years (2005–2012) saw a larger increase in the percentage of expenditures devoted to student services than the first

Table 6.6. Average Dollars per Student Expended on Student Services by Carnegie Classification

	Dollars		
Classification	2001–2002	2005–2006	2011–2012
Associate's	1,125	1,322	1,552
Baccalaureate	2,911	3,786	4,545
Master's	1,863	2,282	2,935
Research	1,686	2,164	2,705

Table 6.7. Percentage of Student Services Expenditures by Institutional Selectivity

	Percentage		
Selectivity	2001–2002	2005–2006	2011–2012
Not Competitive	9.2	9.7	12.5
Less Competitive	11.4	12.5	14.2
Competitive	11.8	12.9	14.3
Very Competitive	10.9	11.7	12.8
Highly Competitive	9.9	10.9	11.5
Most Competitive	8.2	9.0	8.6

5 years. For the most competitive institutions, the percentage of expenditures devoted to student services decreased. However, despite the percentage decrease, the most competitive institutions spend more money on student services per student than their less selective peers. Table 6.8 also mirrors past research illustrating the positive relationship between selectivity and expenditures—the higher the selectivity level, the more money institutions spend per student.

Summary. The previous sections demonstrate that institutions' sources of revenues have altered over the past 2 years but expenditure patterns have remained relatively consistent. Focusing specifically on student services expenditures illustrates that institutional characteristics such as Carnegie Classification and selectivity also play in the percentage of funds allocated to student services as well as the amount. We recognize that making institutional decisions based on these more generalized data is difficult. Nevertheless, because budgets have significant impacts on the work and scope of student affairs, it is critical that student affairs professionals have a more macro level understanding of the higher education revenue and resource allocation landscape.

Table 6.8. Student Services Expenditures per Full-Time Equivalent Student by Institutional Selectivity

	Dollars		
Selectivity	2001–2002	2005–2006	2011–2012
Not Competitive	1,394	1,770	2,599
Less Competitive	1,821	2,289	2,961
Competitive	2,067	2,633	3,260
Very Competitive	2,391	3,051	3,726
Highly Competitive	3,101	4,021	4,887
Most Competitive	4,372	6,016	6,756

Institutional Budget Models

The previous section provided insights on categories of expenditures, revenues, and a glimpse of those expenditures devoted to student services expenditures. This section provides an overview of the budgeting and finance models that guide these decisions and how these models have changed in the past decade.

In a 2011 survey of 606 college and university business officers, five most commonly used budget models were identified: formula, incremental, performance-based, revenue centered management (RCM), and zero-based budgeting (Green et al., 2011). Formula-based funding is simply a model whereby a budget is determined by an agreed-upon formula. The advantages of this model are that it is transparent and can quantify budget increases (Massy, 1996). Incremental funding models require individuals to make the case for increased funding based on certain factors. It starts with the assumption that institutions will receive what they had received in the past (allowing for increases due to salary adjustments, inflation, etc.) but any additional funding needs to be justified.

Performance-based funding models connect funding to institutional performance on specific indicators (Dougherty & Reddy, 2011, 2013). Currently, distinctions have been made between performance funding 1.0 and performance funding 2.0 models. In performance funding 1.0 models, institutions may get a bonus over regular funding. Performance funding 2.0 models put more emphasis on what Dougherty and Reddy (2013) call "indicators of intermediate achievement" (p. 6) such as course completion or student completion in specific types of courses (e.g., mathematics, remedial, etc.). In addition, performance funding 2.0 models no longer provide institutions a bonus in addition to their regular funding but rather are "embedding it in the regular state base funding" (Dougherty & Reddy, 2013, p. 6).

Revenue-centered management (RCM) shifts budgeting decisions to individual units (Strauss, Curry, & Whalen, 1996). Units have the responsibility for generating and spending revenues. To protect other units that may not be able to generate their own resources, a type of "tax" may be required of units. So, for example, at institutions where these models are in place, academic units that can generate revenue through enrollment may be asked to devote a certain percentage of their revenue to student affairs units that are seen as important but unable to generate their own revenue (Strauss et al., 1996).

The final model, zero-based budgeting, is, as it implies, a model where each year the budget starts with zero (Kircher & Enyeart, 2009). It is designed to give units an opportunity to review how they want to allocate their resources. Unlike the incremental budget model where institutions need to provide a rationale only for new funding or programs, this model requires institutions to justify the use of all programs and expenditures.

The 2011 Inside Higher Education Survey asked business officers to compare budget models from 2007 to 2011 (Green et al., 2011). In that time, reliance on formula-based budget (27.1% vs. 26.1%) and incremental-based budget (68.8% vs. 60.2%) models decreased whereas performance-based, RCM, and zero-based budgeting models increased. Performance-based budget models increased more significantly at public, not-for-profit (12.8% vs. 21%) and private, for-profit (11.1 % vs. 22.2%) institutions. The percentage of public, doctoral institutions using a RCM model increased from 6.4% in 2007 to 21.3% in 2011.

The results illustrate that institutions are moving toward models that require units to be more responsible for and transparent with their budgets. This trend is not surprising and mirrors the larger higher education context. Taxpayers, legislatures, governing bodies, and executive administrators are calling for greater accountability within higher education institutions and this call is being reflected in current and changing budget models.

Challenges for Student Affairs Budgeting and Finances

Budgeting and financing of student affairs divisions is undoubtedly affected by the changes in revenue streams, expenditure decisions, and budgeting models. This section describes how student affairs budgeting and finances have also been affected. These themes were identified from a cross-section of Chief Student Affairs Officers (CSAOs) and their budget officers' responses to an inquiry about how the funding of student affairs has changed over the past 20 years. Even among the different types of institutions there was commonality in responses resulting in some consistent themes.

Changes in Student Services Allocation. Chief Student Affairs Officers (CSAOs) cited some changes in the way funding has been allocated to student services functions, some as a result of institutional funding decisions and others internally driven within the student affairs division. It has included presidents' deciding to reallocate directly to student services functions and bypassing the CSAO's discretion. CSAOs have also requested reallocation plans from direct reports and made disproportionate changes in reductions or allocations in contrast to the funding changes coming from central processes. These changes have been driven by shifts in funding levels. Some states have seen economic prosperity and higher education has benefitted. In many states fiscal challenges have had an impact on higher education funding and as a result CSAOs have had to manage reductions.

Educating on the Relevance of Student Affairs. Although not new, educating decision makers on the relevance and contributions of student affairs to the overall institutional mission remains a common challenge among CSAOs. This challenge was present when funding levels were increasing and student affairs sought to secure proportional increases or when resources were declining and student affairs were hoping for proportional reductions similar to, and not more than, academic units within the university.

Using Auxiliary Revenues to Support Other Activities.   When central funding levels are reduced some university leaders and CSAOs have resorted to reallocating auxiliary revenues to support activities and programs previously supported by the general fund. As self-operated units, this raiding of auxiliary funding creates concern for students' view of relative value, which can lead to students choosing not to use the services or, in the case of housing and dining, seeking off-campus alternatives. This shift can result in reduced income but also have unintended consequences related to student outcomes because participating in on-campus housing and activities consistently has been shown to enhance student engagement and persistence.

The second impact of internally reallocating from auxiliaries can be a lack of transparency with students. If students pay for one service, such as housing, but these funds are reallocated to another area, the temptation may be to not disclose that "paying for housing is also paying for student counseling services." This practice can create significant conflict and distrust between students and university leaders.

Increasing or Adding Student Fees.   In addition to reallocating from auxiliaries, some colleges and universities have significantly raised student fees as a way to compensate for general fund reductions. These fees are often approved outside tuition processes and often do not get included in the national dialogue on tuition outpacing inflation. These fee increases do, however, affect total cost of attendance. Student borrowing rates have increased over recent years and all costs including tuition, student fees, and room and board have received much more attention than in previous years. This strategy appears to be waning in light of the national conversation.

Participating in Fundraising.   For many CSAOs the opportunity, and often necessity, to partner with their foundation for annual and endowment funding is a new responsibility. Numerous student affairs central office websites connect prospective donors with core student life experiences that created lifelong connections to their undergraduate experiences.

For decades, academics and athletics were given first priority at soliciting from donors wishing to make a difference by investing in education. As many universities became more donor centered in their investigation of donor wishes, they learned there was a tremendous opportunity to enhance the likelihood donors would give by identifying the deep connections to their student life experiences. Greek life, leadership involvement, multicultural support programs, and many other student affairs functions created deep connections for many students that now translate or could be translated into scholarship funding, new buildings, and endowed funding for activities that sustain student life programs. Although many CSAOs are directly involved in foundation work, many are now hiring development directors to work specifically on behalf of student services programs.

Strategies Informing Student Affairs Resource Allocation

There are many factors—internal and external to the institution—that influence revenues and expenditure decisions. Although not everything is within the control of the student affairs administrator, we offer some strategies that can inform budget decisions and help minimize the challenges associated with changing budgetary and financial environments.

Focus on Mission. In an era of constant change, one piece of advice remains the same: focus on the mission. In their study of high-impact institutions, *Student Success in College: Creating Conditions That Matter*, Kuh, Kinzie, Schuh, and Whitt (2010) stress that institutions that could articulate their mission and used this to guide decisions were most successful in affecting student learning. This principle applies to resource allocation decisions as well. Know your mission, your strengths, and your values and allocate resources accordingly.

Know Key Decision Makers. Despite assertions that formulas and models drive funding decisions, the reality is people make these decisions. Many CSAOs stated it has been critical for them to understand what is relevant to key decision makers—presidents, trustees, chancellors, legislators, or donors—regarding what demands appropriate resourcing. This has occurred through direct inquiry about how student affairs would be measured or over time as proposals were presented and received approval, disapproval, or no action.

Show Them the Data. For many decision makers, key performance indicators and data points may be the cornerstone to influencing funding changes for student service functions. Many university leaders want to see demonstrated and substantial impacts before making funding allocations or reallocations. Anecdotes and previous ways of operating provide little convincing evidence. Invest in reliable and accessible data management systems and hire and train individuals to use these systems in order to make data-driven decisions. If it can be demonstrated that programs positively contribute to an institution's goals and mission, these programs may be spared even when revenues are declining. Conversely, high-impact programs are likely to receive additional funding under revenue growth periods.

Engage in Assessment. In addition to collecting data, it is critical that student affairs professionals engage in the larger process of assessment. Gathering data points, benchmarking, and providing key performance indicators are important, but equally important is engaging in the process of assessment. Although data collection is an aspect of assessment, assessment requires student affairs members to articulate goals and purposes and collect and analyze data to evaluate whether these goals are being met, and subsequently, make decisions based on these data (Maki, 2010). Assessment is a reflective process that can provide insights into resource allocation decisions.

Use the Voice and Experiences of Students.   As student affairs professionals, use the voices of your students. Student testimonials and advocacy can have a powerful impact on decision makers. Student leaders who understand and have directly experienced the benefits of student services can be tremendous ambassadors during the process of allocating resources. At many universities, student leaders such as those serving on student government boards enjoy much more frequent and candid access to decision makers than many student affairs staff experience. The conversations that occur in these conditions can create a great foundation for substantiating the validity of formal requests.

Understand Your Past to Assist the Present and Future.   There are decades of evidence that funding for higher education and student affairs is dynamic and demands constant attention by leaders within student affairs. Sufficient information exists on historical changes in environmental conditions for savvy leaders to use to their advantage. If CSAOs understand how historical factors have influenced funding levels, they can anticipate and capitalize on this knowledge as they navigate processes and people to best serve their divisions. Understanding leadership changes, the political dynamics on the horizon, and how historical fluctuations in the economy, like recessions, affect higher education and serve as predictors to future funding are central to effective student affairs leadership.

Conclusion

The first decade of the 21st century has seen significant changes in higher education. Schuh's (2003) prediction made over 10 years ago may perhaps be even more accurate in today's environment: The financial environment is challenging and this challenge is likely to continue. The piece of hope, however, is that many institutions have found a way to overcome these challenges. Focusing on mission; using data, assessment, and student voices; and being aware of the historical context and present decision makers, student affairs administrators will rise to these challenges and continue to garner the resources necessary to provide high-quality learning and support student success.

References

Barron's Educational Series. (2009). *2009 Barron's profiles of American colleges* (28th ed.). Hauppauge, NY: Barron's Educational Series.

Bowen, W. G., Chingos, M. M., & McPherson, M. S. (2009). *Crossing the finish line: Completing college at America's public universities.* Princeton, NJ: University Press.

Dougherty, K. J., & Reddy, V. (2011). *The impacts of state performance funding systems on higher education institutions: Research literature review and policy recommendations* (CCRC Working Paper No. 37). New York, NY: Columbia University, Teachers College.

Dougherty, K. J., & Reddy, V. (Eds.). (2013). *Performance funding for higher education: What are the mechanisms? What are the impacts?* (ASHE Higher Education Report, Vol. 39, No. 2). San Francisco, CA: Jossey-Bass.

Gansemer-Topf, A. M., & Schuh, J. H. (2006). Institutional selectivity and institutional expenditures: Examining organizational factors that contribute to retention and graduation. *Research in Higher Education, 47*(6), 613–642.

Green, K. C., Jaschik, S., & Lederman, D. (2011). *The 2011 Inside Higher Ed survey of college & university business officers.* Retrieved from https://www.insidehighered.com /news/survey/maintenance-over-management-survey-business-officers

Green, K. C., Jaschik, S., & Lederman, D. (2012). *The 2012 Inside Higher Ed survey of college & university business officers.* Retrieved from https://www.insidehighered.com /news/survey/short-term-focus-long-term-problems-survey-business-officers

Jaschik, S., & Lederman, D. (2013). *The 2013 Inside Higher Ed survey of college & university business officers.* Retrieved from https://www.insidehighered.com /news/survey/cfo-survey-reveals-doubts-about-financial-sustainability

Kircher, A., & Enyeart, C. (2009). *The use of zero-based budgeting in higher education.* Washington, DC: Advisory Board Company. Retrieved from http://www4.uwm .edu/secu/faculty/standing/apbc/agendas/11-12/upload/The_Use_of_Zero-Based _Budgeting_in_Higher_Education-1.pdf

Kuh, G. D., Kinzie, J., Schuh, J. H., & Whitt, E. J. (2010). *Student success in college: Creating conditions that matter.* San Francisco, CA: Jossey-Bass.

Maki, P. L. (2010). *Assessing for learning: Building a sustainable commitment across the institution.* Sterling, VA: Stylus Publishing.

Massy, W. F. (1996). Reengineering resource allocation systems. In W. F. Massy (Ed.), *Resource allocation in higher education* (pp. 15–47). Ann Arbor: The University of Michigan Press.

National Center for Education Statistics (NCES). (2008a). *Digest of Education Statistics: Table 350. Revenues of public degree-granting institutions, by source of revenue and type of institution: 2003–04, 2004–05, and 2005–06.* Retrieved from http://nces.ed.gov/programs/digest/d08/tables/dt08_350.asp

National Center for Education Statistics (NCES). (2008b). *Digest of Education Statistics: Table 362. Expenditures of public degree-granting institutions, by purpose of expenditure and type of institution: 2003–04, 2004–05, and 2005–06.* Retrieved from http://nces.ed.gov/programs/digest/d08/tables/dt08_362.asp

National Center for Education Statistics (NCES). (2013a). *Digest of Education Statistics: Table 333.10. Revenues of public degree-granting postsecondary institutions, by source of revenue and level of institution: 2005-06 through 2011-12.* Retrieved from http://nces.ed.gov/programs/digest/d13/tables/dt13_333.10.asp

National Center for Education Statistics (NCES). (2013b). *Digest of Education Statistics: Table 333.40. Total revenue of private nonprofit degree-granting postsecondary institutions, by source of funds and level of institution: 1999-2000 through 2011-12.* Retrieved from http://nces.ed.gov/programs/digest/d13/tables/dt13_333.40.asp

National Center for Education Statistics (NCES). (2013c). *Digest of Education Statistics: Table 334.10. Expenditures of public degree-granting postsecondary institutions, by purpose of expenditure and level of institution: 2005-06 through 2011-12.* Retrieved from http://nces.ed.gov/programs/digest/d13/tables/dt13_334.10.asp

National Center for Education Statistics (NCES). (2013d). *Digest of Education Statistics: Table 334.30. Total expenditures of private nonprofit degree-granting postsecondary institutions, by purpose and level of institution: 1999-2000 through 2011-12.* Retrieved from http://nces.ed.gov/programs/digest/d13/tables/dt13_334.30.asp

Schuh, J. H. (2003). The financial environment of student affairs. In J. H. Schuh (Ed.), *New Directions for Student Services: No. 103. Contemporary financial issues in student affairs* (pp. 3–16). San Francisco, CA: Jossey-Bass.

Strauss, J., Curry, J., & Whalen, E. (1996). Revenue responsibility budgeting. In W. F. Massy (Ed.), *Resource allocation in higher education* (pp. 163–190). Ann Arbor: University of Michigan Press.

Titus, M. A. (2006). Understanding college degree completion of students with low socioeconomic status: The influence of institutional financial context. *Research in Higher Education, 47*(4), 371–378.

U.S. Department of Education. (2009). *State fiscal stabilization fund.* Retrieved from http://www2.ed.gov/policy/gen/leg/recovery/factsheet/stabilization-fund.html

ANN M. GANSEMER-TOPF *is assistant professor in the School of Education at Iowa State University.*

PETER D. ENGLIN *is director of residence and former dean of students at Iowa State University.*

Changes in the preparation of student affairs educators are described and discussed in this chapter.

Preparing Student Affairs Educators

Anna M. Ortiz, Ilinca Filimon, Monica Cole-Jackson

Since 1996, graduate preparation for the profession of student affairs has changed in many key ways. For example, since 1996 we have seen a dramatic increase in the number and size of preparation programs, as well as in the diversity of students in those programs. Indeed, according to the American College Personnel Association (ACPA) program directory, the number of student affairs preparation programs has almost doubled since 1997. In addition, what is considered "the canon"—those components of curricula and experiences regarded generally as essential to effective student affairs preparation—has changed to reflect the expanding diversity of students entering college and the expanding diversity of the nature of what is meant by "college." Theories and studies of college students, for example, include topics and students that were not likely to be studied or written about in 1996.

Also, electronic technologies have transformed nearly all aspects of graduate student affairs preparation. In 1996, e-mail was not taken for granted throughout higher education as a way for students to communicate with faculty and staff, nor was ready access to online resources or social media. Today, the Internet is a place not only for easy access to scholarship but also to deliver and receive learning. As educational and online technologies have exploded, so have professional development opportunities for all student affairs professionals. No longer do the major professional associations offer just single annual conferences. Now there are conferences focused on increasingly specific functional areas, needs of different professional levels of responsibility, and student affairs work at different types of institutions. In addition, technology has enabled professional development via multiple modalities and allows for almost instantaneous training and development in addressing current issues.

In this chapter we review these and other changes in graduate student affairs preparation by reviewing professional documents, graduate preparation textbooks, and literature and by examining the many opportunities available on the worldwide web. For example, we drew on the National

New Directions for Student Services, no. 151, Fall 2015 © 2015 Wiley Periodicals, Inc.
Published online in Wiley Online Library (wileyonlinelibrary.com) • DOI: 10.1002/ss.20139

Student Affairs Archives housed at Bowling Green State University to obtain syllabi from 1997 to the present and for courses such as introduction to student affairs, multicultural issues in higher education, and student development theories. We also analyzed past and current graduate program directories from National Association of Student Personnel Administrators (NASPA) and ACPA.

We also conducted a small research project, the results of which are described here. In fall 2014, research participants were recruited via *CSPTalk*, a listserv for graduate preparation faculty, to receive a survey using the online tool *Qualtrics*. To be included in the study, participants had to have been teaching in a student affairs graduate preparation program in 1996 and in 2014. Most of the 22 participants were part-time or adjunct instructors or assistant professors in 1996; in 2014, most were full professors, associate professors, or assistant professors. Most participants were employed at public institutions; most of those institutions enrolled 10,000–30,000 students. We collected data about the faculty members' backgrounds and institutions and used open-ended questions to ask them to compare and contrast their experiences teaching in a graduation preparation program (all but one participant teach at both the master's and doctoral level) in 1996 with their experiences in 2014. We also asked them speculate how graduate student affairs preparation might change in the future.

Major Changes in Master's-Level Preparation

This section describes major changes in master's-level preparation, including graduate program enrollments, curricula, experiential options, and accreditation and professional competencies.

Graduate Program Enrollments. According to the 1999 American College Personnel Association graduate program directory, 82 colleges and universities in the United States offered student affairs graduate programs with degrees including master of arts, master of science, and master of education. Today, the ACPA directory lists 157 institutions of higher education that offer student affairs graduate preparation programs. Although this list is longer than that from 1999, it is not exhaustive, as ACPA requires a subscription fee and the submission of a Council for the Advancement of Standards in Higher Education (CAS) standards self-study for inclusion in the directory.

The National Association of Student Personnel Administrators has also compiled a directory of graduate programs in higher education organized by areas of focus (i.e., administration, counseling, leadership, and student learning and development). Although student affairs is not included as a focus, we concluded from our examination of the programs listed in the directory that 142 of those programs included elements of what we consider to be a "typical" student affairs graduate program. The titles of the majors in the 142 ranged from student development in higher education to higher education with an emphasis in student affairs to college student personnel. This list, too, is extensive, but not exhaustive as inclusion in the directory and regular updates are at the discretion of the programs. We concluded, then, from our analysis of directories of student affairs graduate preparation programs from 1999 to 2014 that the number of these programs has nearly doubled in that period of time. Although these programs differ in length, type of degree, and title, they appear to share the goal of preparing graduate students to work effectively with college students in a variety of roles and at a variety of types of institutions.

Curricula. Curricular changes from 1996 to present in graduate preparation programs differ depending on the source of data about those changes. According to our analysis of program directories and syllabi, the curriculum for most programs today is similar to what one would have found in 1996. That is, program curricula continue to be organized into foundation courses (e.g., theories of student development, principles of student affairs practice, history of higher education), professional studies (e.g., research methods, specializations in student affairs), supervised practice (e.g., internships, practica), elective courses, and, in some cases, counseling courses. Program information and syllabi from 1996 show increasing attention to diversity (e.g., in research on student development), but today's data show a broader and more complex focus on social justice and multiculturalism, as well as diversity.

When asked how curricula have changed in graduate preparation programs since 1996, our survey participants reported more dramatic changes in programs than we found in our document analysis. The most common descriptors of program emphasis in 1996 were (in order of frequency) counseling, administration, and student development. When asked about curricula in 2014, most respondents identified two main foci: student development (alone or combined with administration) and social justice (or similar terms). Only two respondents identified counseling as a current program emphasis.

When asked about changes in work assigned in courses, survey participants reported many similarities between 1996 and today. Typical assignments, then and now, include expectations for reading and class participation, reviews of literature, group projects and presentations, and professional and personal reflections. However, respondents noted a shift to more practical and applied assignments, portfolio development, projects focused on conducting research and assessment, and even greater use of reflections.

Perhaps the biggest differences between 1996 and 2014 noted by our survey respondents are in pedagogies they use to implement the curriculum. Changes in teaching and learning were attributed to changes in instructional technologies, as well as in student characteristics and experiences. Learning Management Systems and other technologies are used widely in instruction and in assignments. Discussion boards, the development of instructional videos to supplement in-class activities, "flipped" classrooms, synchronous and asynchronous *chatting*, and the use of services such as Skype or Camtasia to bring students and guest experts into the classroom or virtual spaces are increasingly typical approaches. Although the traditional lecture continues to be a part of the instructor toolbox, faculty–student-centered discussions and collaborative learning activities were reported as the primary pedagogical strategies used today.

Survey participants also noted changes over the past 18 years in their teaching and overall experiences in professional preparation as a result of changes they perceive in their master's students. Many of the respondents find that students are coming to them less prepared for graduate-level work, particularly in regard to writing. However, they also see students less prepared interpersonally and intrapersonally. One faculty member stated students are "emotionally immature and are unable to work with uncertainty," whereas another characterized students as "less independent, they require more structure and guidance as they enter." One faculty member speculated that a need for structure may be connected to the context in which they grew up: "They crave structure, they are fearful with lots of worries about guns/shooters, crises on campus, major disasters. You can tell they are products of Columbine, 9/11, the Oklahoma bombing, and perpetual war." Some faculty felt lower levels of maturity and need for more structure and less ambiguity require more effort from faculty in teaching and advising than in the past. For some, this comes at the expense of scholarly and grant productivity.

However, respondents also find that their students are far more comfortable with people who are different from themselves and are "more sophisticated and confident in their knowledge of multicultural issues." One said, "They are way more interested in veterans, students with disabilities, and international students than 20 years ago." This, too, has required a change in pedagogy, as respondents said they need to prepare differently for approaching social justice as "a core philosophy" and for students who "are prepared to have higher level discussions. They are especially interested in topics around identity development and willing to read, research, and discuss topics (orientation, ability, race, gender, class) that in 1996 those students did not do willingly."

Our survey participants also described their students as being more focused on the development of specific job skills, especially in functional areas outside of residence life, sometimes at the expense of gaining a deep understanding of the course content. They also reported that students are coming into master's programs with fewer leadership experiences and involvement as undergraduates, which has caused an increase in the use of applied assignments and a push for more experiential options in programs.

Experiential Options.   According to the NASPA program directory, all graduate student affairs programs offer assistantships, fellowships, scholarships, and/or financial aid to help defray the cost of tuition, fees, and related educational costs. In 1996, the graduate assistantship in residence life was the primary experiential option that was used to fund students and to prepare future professionals. These assistantships no longer play such a central role as many programs use an array of employment options and graduate placements to train students and fund the degree. Increasingly, for example, master's students are employed in research fellowships or serve as research assistants.

Almost all master's programs require a supervised internship (usually nonpaid) as a part of the curriculum. These internships range from 100 hours to the entire length of the program. Internships typically are part of an academic course that focuses on what students are learning in their field-work and how what they are learning relates to their other coursework and assistantship experiences. Types of internships and diversity of placements also have increased since 1996. Programs partner with neighboring institutions to provide internships in diverse institutional types. Professional associations offer summer internships that allow students to gain experience across the country. International options are organized by individual programs, host countries, and higher education institutions or by students themselves.

Given the expansion of experiential options in the past 18 years, we were not surprised that our survey respondents reported that the biggest change they have witnessed in the employment of their graduates is the diversity of positions and functional areas they choose. They find that more of their graduates seek their first professional position in advising than residence life, for example. However, students who go this route may have more difficulty getting that first position, especially before graduation (having a job at the time of graduation seemed to be the norm in 1996). Several respondents mentioned that, although they have not seen a decrease in employment rates of their graduates, they have seen an increase in the amount of time it takes for graduates to find a job. One faculty member explained:

Employment appears to more challenging . . . I'm not sure if that is due to fewer jobs, more graduates or if people are more geographically limited. In 1996, my graduate students seemed more eager to try a new place or a new kind of campus. More and more today, my graduates are focused on being near family or a significant other so their job options appear limited.

Accreditation and Professional Competencies. Accreditation for student affairs graduate preparation programs is limited to the 30 programs accredited by the Council for Accreditation for Counseling and Related Educational Programs (CACREP). In general, counseling-focused graduate preparation programs have decreased in number and popularity as programs have taken on more of an emphasis on student development, administration, and social justice. The Council for the Advancement of Standards in Higher Education (CAS) published standards for the academic preparation of student affairs professionals in 1986. These standards have guided the development, change, and assessment of many graduate preparation programs. As mentioned previously, entry to the ACPA Directory of Graduate Programs is predicated on self-assessment using the CAS Standards (CAS, 2006). Recently, ACPA and NASPA developed a set of professional competencies, which were published in a joint document in 2010 (ACPA & NASPA, 2010). These 10 areas of competency define competence according to professional level (basic, intermediate, and advanced). Nearly every faculty respondent in our study noted that they use these competencies to guide curriculum development and use them as an indication of what competencies graduates should demonstrate in the future.

Doctoral Preparation

Although there is continual growth in the discipline of Student Affairs and Higher Education Administration (SA-HE), growth in doctoral preparation has been more limited than that at the master's level. According to the NASPA program directory, there are only 23 in-residence and 18 blended or online terminal degree programs in SA-HE (NASPA, 2014). Many doctoral programs that have prepared student affairs leaders (75% of chief student affairs officers hold the degree) have a more general higher education focus or an even more general educational leadership curriculum. Therefore, focusing specifically on student affairs underestimates the number of doctoral programs relevant to this chapter. Nevertheless, more senior-level student affairs administrators hold terminal degrees in SA-HE in 2014 than 20 years ago.

A terminal degree can be seen as an advantage in obtaining a leadership position in student affairs. For example, Howard-Hamilton and Hyman (2009) asserted that, "without a doctorate many administrators remain in entry or mid-level positions" (p. 390). Others have posited the expectation that student affairs leaders hold a terminal degree to effectively carry out the positions' duties is not supported by evidence (Reason, Walker, & Robinson, 2002). These assertions are not contradictory, however. Claiming that student affairs professionals need terminal degrees to advance into leadership positions is not the same as claiming terminal degrees are necessary to be effective in those positions.

Table 7.1 notes changes over time in the number and nature of terminal degrees held by chief student affairs officers (typically, vice presidents, vice chancellors, or vice provosts for student affairs; Wesaw & Sponsler, 2014).

The faculty members we surveyed reported that doctoral programs in higher education and student affairs have become bifurcated by purpose and intended outcomes since 1996. One noted, for example, a "gap between part-time web-based programs for practitioners and full-time on-campus programs for those intending to be faculty." With regard to the former, respondents expressed concern about the increase in short-term executive

Table 7.1. Terminal Degree Held by Chief Student Affairs Officers

Decade	Student Affairs Professionals With Terminal Degree	Student Affairs Professionals With Terminal Degree in Student or Higher Education Administration
1994	39%	25%
2000	56%	52%
2014	56%	75%

programs that "are becoming profit centers, online programs that may or may not teach needed skills and offer mentoring in the profession." Respondents also perceive a "move toward management skills instead of theory." One asserted, however, that, for preparation for student affairs work, "student affairs degrees at the master's level are sufficient. Doctoral programs should be based on broader 'higher education' concepts to understand the university system as a whole: finance, policy analysis, legal/political theory/application, organization and governance, administration and leadership theory/application."

Survey participants also perceived doctoral programs whose aim is to prepare faculty and scholars are increasingly accepting students straight out of master's programs. Respondents fear this practice is leading to faculty members in graduate preparation programs who have little or no professional experience in student affairs and, perhaps, little teaching experience. This is a concern given the role master's programs play in the professional development of student affairs practitioners. Participants suggested that doctoral programs require some level of professional experience and take care to develop teachers as well as scholars.

Two additional developments in doctoral education since 1996 were noted by the faculty respondents: (a) widespread acceptance of the use of qualitative research methods for dissertations and other scholarship, and (b) the growth in the number of student affairs and higher education faculty in both small and large programs. At the same time, however, they wished for more changes in global emphases in doctoral programs, including coursework in comparative education and opportunities for international study.

Trends in Professional Development

In addition to earning a master's or doctoral degree in student affairs or higher education, student affairs staff at all levels and in all areas can choose from a plethora of professional development opportunities to support professional effectiveness and career mobility. Professional development opportunities have exploded since 1996 as professional organizations have matured and diversified and as the Internet has allowed for professional development webinars and publications. Faculty members in our survey felt that there are so many professional opportunities that graduate students and new professionals are pulled in a number of directions and are even at risk of being lured by—in the words of one respondent—"proprietary workshops on student affairs topics with hefty price tags that seem exploitive to new professionals."

Professional development includes international study trips to expand global awareness and competence, as well as to promote multinational partnerships. Professional development also has been demonstrated to improve job satisfaction of entry-level staff members, as well as to reduce attrition of professionals from the field (Tull, 2006).

One of the areas of competency that has, perhaps, changed the most in demand and sophistication in student affairs since 1996 is assessment, evaluation, and research. Expectations that student affairs units will engage in rigorous outcomes assessment, evaluation of program effectiveness, and data-driven decision making have increased across institutions of higher education as resources have become more scarce, calls for accountability more common, and research regarding effective student affairs practice more widely disseminated. According to our faculty respondents, professional development has been the primary vehicle for teaching these skills, but many also reported that this has been an area of growth in graduate program curricula in recent decades.

The Future of Graduate Preparation

The pace of change we have seen in student affairs graduate preparation over the past decades must continue—even, perhaps, accelerate. New and rapidly changing electronic and instructional technologies and the challenges and opportunities they pose for student affairs work are addressed in Chapter 5 of this sourcebook; suffice it to say here that these changes will affect graduate preparation, both in ways we can anticipate and in those we cannot. Similarly dramatic changes in what constitutes a college education—where it takes place and under what circumstances, for example—also demand new ways of thinking about what constitutes student affairs work. And all of these changes have implications for services, resources, policies, and practices. Perhaps the most important role for graduate programs in this environment of quick and constant change is preparing student affairs professionals to have a clear sense of values and purpose with regard to students and their success, as well as the mission of their institutions, to work well under conditions of ambiguity, and to take an inquiry-oriented approach to their tasks so they can learn quickly and respond effectively to the changes they face.

Research has indicated chief student affairs officers spend most of their time on four tasks: (a) administration, (b) personnel, (c) interactions with students, and (d) strategic planning and crisis management (Wesaw & Sponsler, 2014). Therefore, graduate program curricula should prepare students for such tasks, including opportunities to learn how to respond effectively to crises.

In addition, addressing the contemporary needs of an increasingly diverse student population involves new and dynamic decision making, including with regard to campus climate; changing student demographics; diversity, equity, and inclusion; and campus safety. For example, student populations in some states are vested with new rights related to legalized marijuana use and legalized same-sex marriage that have wide-ranging issues for policies, practices, and programs.

The faculty respondents in our study identified many of these topics when asked how graduate preparation needed to change to prepare graduates to meet the challenges and opportunities of the future. They added that graduate students needed to also learn how to collaborate with academic affairs units and decrease discourse about the divide between academic and student affairs. One connected this to assessment's increasing role in the profession: "To teach assessment to better justify the importance of student affairs is critical, along with exposure of students to academic administrators to model collaboration." How do programs address these needs? When asked what content or courses would need to be emphasized to meet these needs, nearly every area was mentioned by at least one participant. They could not identify any content or courses that would be obsolete in the future, leaving one to conclude, "we will be pushed to add more."

Indeed, there seemed to be a concern about the health of the programs in the future as the faculty respondents reported increasing competition among programs. Many called for an enactment of regulations to ensure that standards are met across programs, with one specifically calling for "marginal programs to be regulated out of existence." This sentiment aligns with the relative frequent calls for accreditation in both student affairs divisions and graduate programs.

The future of professional preparation is in the hands of our faculty. They direct and create curricula, they admit candidates into programs, they serve as the constant in the preparation through teaching, mentoring, and advising. Because many graduate students are supervised by relatively new professionals, faculty members are critical in the socialization of professionals. In order to meet the demands of the next 20 years, faculty will need to increase their work with chief student affairs officers and other campus leaders to ensure that students are learning the content and skills that meet the needs of the profession. Because 50% of CSAOs are between 50 and 60 years old, White, and male (Wesaw & Sponsler, 2014), the professionals we prepare now in our master's and doctoral programs will diversify and shape the profession to serve a student body that has changed dramatically since 1996, where crisis management reflects the complex world in which we live, and where students come to our campuses with experiences and needs that we largely have not seen in higher education. Graduate preparation program continue to be ready to meet the challenge.

References

American College Personnel Association (ACPA) & National Association of Student Personnel Administrators (NASPA). (2010). *Professional competency areas for student affairs practitioners*. Retrieved from http://www.naspa.org/images/uploads /main/Professional_Competencies.pdf

Council for the Advancement of Standards in Higher Education (CAS). (2006). *CAS professional standards for higher education* (6th ed.). Washington, DC: Author.

Howard-Hamilton, M. F., & Hyman, R. E. (2009). Doctoral education and beyond. In G. S. McClellan, G. S. J. Stringer, & Associates (Eds.), *The handbook of student affairs administration* (2nd ed., pp. 388–402). San Francisco, CA: Jossey-Bass.

National Association of Student Personnel Administrators (NASPA). (2014). *Graduate program directory search*. Retrieved December 10, 2014, from http://apps.naspa .org/gradprograms/search.cfm

Reason, R. D., Walker, D. A., & Robinson, D. C. (2002). Gender, ethnicity, and highest degree earned as salary determinants for senior student affairs officers at public institutions. *NASPA Journal, 39*(3), 251–265.

Tull, A. (2006). Synergistic supervision, job satisfaction, and intention to turnover of new professionals in student affairs. *Journal of College Student Development, 47*(4), 465–480. doi:10.1353/csd.2006.0053

Wesaw, A. J., & Sponsler, B. A. (2014). *The chief student affairs officer: Responsibilities, opinions, and professional pathways of leaders in student affairs*. Washington, DC: NASPA Research and Policy Institute.

Anna M. Ortiz *is professor and department chair of educational leadership at Long Beach State University.*

Ilinca Filimon *is a graduate student in counseling with an option in student development in higher education at Long Beach State University.*

Monica Cole-Jackson *is a doctoral student at Long Beach State University.*

8

Based on experiences over the past 2 decades, the authors look at some of the challenges of making predictions and then offer some thoughts about student affairs practice in the foreseeable future.

Peering Into the Future

Elizabeth J. Whitt, John H. Schuh

The bulk of this volume has been devoted to the observations and conclusions of our chapter authors about what has transpired in a number of important aspects of student affairs practice over the past 18 years. We took a look at the content of the 70 or so volumes we published and then asked chapter authors to look at such elements of student affairs work as effective practice, characteristics of students, assessment, budgeting and finance, and the use of technology in an effort to trace the developments of the past 2 decades of student affairs practice.

To conclude this volume we make some guesses about what we think might be the future of student affairs practice for the next 10 or even 15 years. This activity is complicated as we attempt to predict what student affairs practice might look like to meet the needs of students far into the future; at the far end of this range the college students of the future are still in elementary school. We can predict one aspect of the future with absolute certainty: We won't be editing this series past 2016!

Looking ahead to what the future of student affairs might hold over the next decade or two can be a bit risky, if not downright dangerous, for one's reputation, because predictions can go awry. Both long-term trends as well as intervening events influence the future in ways that are difficult to predict. As an illustration, support from state governments for public universities has been in an inexorable decline for more than 3 decades. From 1980 to 2000 state appropriations as a percentage of current fund revenue for public degree-granting institutions declined from 44.0% to 31.9% (Snyder, Dillow, & Hoffman, 2009, Table 349). Whereas the decline was just a few percentage points most years, over the 20-year period of time the percentage was nearly 30%. Most recently, the decline in constant 2012 dollars was from $9,102 per full-time equivalent (FTE) student in 2005–2006 to $7,970 per FTE student in 2010–2011 (Snyder & Dillow, 2013, Table 401). In the middle of the decline it might have been easy to say, "We'll make up for this year's decline in next year's budget." But the fact is that

NEW DIRECTIONS FOR STUDENT SERVICES, no. 151, Fall 2015 © 2015 Wiley Periodicals, Inc.
Published online in Wiley Online Library (wileyonlinelibrary.com) • DOI: 10.1002/ss.20140

once in long-term decline, it is difficult, if not impossible, to make up for dollars that were lost. In short, once a trend such as this one develops momentum, it is very difficult to stop the momentum and reverse the direction of the trend. And, in the process, assumptions and expectations based on past behavior were not helpful to predict the future.

In other circumstances, a historic event can have a significant influence on how organizations and institutions function. Most dramatic in this century were the events of September 11, 2001, which changed many aspects of life in the United States and around the world and resulted in the deployment of troops to the Middle East by many nations, more stringent checks on passengers before embarking on airline travel, the formation of the Department of Homeland Security, and so on. Similar dramatic events occurred in the previous century, including the stock market crash in 1929, the attack on Pearl Harbor in 1941, the Cuban Missile Crisis in 1962, and the Chernobyl accident in 1986. Other dramatic events have occurred throughout history that resulted in significant and substantial changes in how people lived their lives. The extent to which any of these events could have been predicted with confidence is a matter for debate, which brings us back to the riskiness of predictions.

It is the case that, sometimes, predictions can be relatively accurate, though they may miss a trend that has a significant influence on the end product. In 2002 the annual *Projections of Education Statistics to 2011* estimated enrollment in degree-granting institutions to be approximately 17,457,000 in 2010–2011 (Hussar, 2002, p. 4). Actual enrollment in degree granting institutions, according to Snyder and Dillow (2013, Table 222) was 21,016,126. Although this projection was short by more than three million, the economic turmoil that at least in part resulted in more individuals enrolling in degree-granting programs than anticipated could not have been predicted in 2002. In addition, the rise of degree-granting for-profit institutions contributed to this enrollment growth. These institutions grew from an enrollment of under 600,000 in 2002 to over 2 million in 2010 (Snyder & Dillow, 2013, Table 222).

Other predictions range from the very accurate (homes that are completely climate controlled) to the extremely inaccurate (television sets ranging from the size of matchboxes to an entire wall) (Bell, 2013). Know anyone who has traveled in a jet at a speed of 2000 miles per hour or lives in a 100-story apartment building? We do not, though these developments were predicted in 1967 (Bell, 2013). So, we realize that making predictions is at best guesswork, perhaps informed by the facts of today but surely risky business.

In some respects, every book or monograph published for a practitioner or graduate student audience in student affairs is a set of predictions, in that the authors include information that they think is important for the readers to know as they prepare for or engage in the practice of student affairs. In effect, they are saying, from the universe of available information, here is what we think is important for you to know as you go forward in your professional practice. Sometimes those predictions are identified, such as in the fifth edition of *Student Services* where the authors (Jones, Harper, & Schuh, 2013) not only described what they thought would be student affairs practice in the future, they also made a number of predictions about the role and identity of student affairs in the future. Although we view some of their predictions as being quite accurate, for example, advocating for rigorous preparation for student affairs staff for diversity, their recommendation that higher education form more partnerships with K–12 schools and communities appears not to be adopted in student affairs practices as widely as the authors advocated.

Our principal professional organizations, the American College Personnel Association and the National Association of Student Personnel Administrators, have also made predictions in recent years (Task Force on the Future of Student Affairs, 2010). The conclusions of the joint Task Force on the Future of Student Affairs mirrored a number of those of Jones, Harper, and Schuh (2013) including increasing globalization, using data to make decisions, working to foster the success of all students, and redesigning student affairs roles and structures. Whether the overlap in these predictions reflects unanimity of thinking or simply coincidence is unknown. Or, it may be that there is consensus among student practitioners and educators, and as a consequence, the future is relatively clear.

Change in Student Affairs

We submit that, in student affairs, some changes occur relatively gradually, but other changes have been quick and profound. Through this sourcebook we have asked our contributors to identify changes in the specific topics for which they were responsible, so, for example, Gansemer-Topf and Englin (Chapter 6) identify the slowly increasing reliance of institutions on tuition and fees as sources of income with expenditures on activities under the umbrella of student affairs changing ever so slightly, though the mix of the expenditures, not captured in National Center for Education Statistics data, may be changing. Cabellon and Junco (Chapter 5), on the other hand, identify rapid changes in technology that are shaping student affairs practice of the future. Instagram, Twitter, and Facebook were not part of student affairs practice when we began our editorial roles; they are now. Who saw these developments coming? Not us, to be sure! Conceding therefore, that our crystal ball may not be any clearer than anyone else's, and perhaps murkier than some, we offer a few guesses as to how student affairs practice might or might not change as we look forward for a decade or two.

Changes Regarding Students.   We start our predictions with students. It's probably safe to "predict" that more people will attend college, leading to enrollments growing at a rate faster than the growth of the population, and that these new students will reflect increasing racial, ethnic, and economic diversity. As this country continues to strive to educate a larger percentage of the population, colleges and universities will have to admit more students who have backgrounds that are different from those who historically have pursued a college education. The trend in this direction already has been well established, in that the percentage of students 18 to 24 years old of all racial groups enrolling in college has increased from 1967 through 2011, though for some groups the growth has been uneven (for example, Pacific Islanders, American Indians, and Alaska Natives, and students of two or more races; Snyder & Dillow, 2013, Table 239). But the trend over decades is unmistakable and we anticipate it will continue for the foreseeable future.

We also believe that the percentage of low-income students who enroll in college will grow, but we are mindful that the odds are very much against these students. The gap in the percentage enrollment of students from low-income families who enroll in postsecondary education when compared with students from middle income and higher income families has been chronic (Silver, 2014). It is also important to note that students graduating from high schools that have a 76–100% participation rate in free or reduced price lunch programs (a proxy for financial need) are less likely to graduate from high school and attend college than their peers who attend high schools that enroll a lower percentage of students who participate in free or reduced-cost lunch programs (Snyder & Dillow, 2013, Table 237). Nevertheless, we are hopeful that a higher percentage of low-income students will enroll in higher education in the future as a result of economic development initiatives by individual states and universities.

Continued growth in international student enrollment as international economies improve is likely. The United States is seen as a destination for students seeking high-quality higher education experiences and if past is prologue, international students will continue to pursue higher education in the United States. From 1980–1981 through 2010–2011, for example, international enrollment grew by more than 400,000 according to the 2012 *Digest of Education Statistics* (Snyder & Dillow, 2013, Table 262).

We anticipate that the percentage of students with disabilities, an often overlooked and frequently marginalized group of students (Myers, Lindburg, & Nied, 2013), will remain about where it is according to the most recent data available. Eleven percent of undergraduates in both 2003–2004 and 2007–2008 reported having a disability (Snyder & Dillow, 2013, Table 269). In 2007–2008, some 43% of undergraduates with disabilities were male and 57% were female, the same percentages as for undergraduates without disabilities.

We also anticipate limited growth in the number of veterans enrolling in colleges and universities. Although this number has experienced growth over the past years, with the drawdown of troops deployed in the Middle East and cuts in real growth in budgets for the armed forces, we anticipate that the size of armed forces will shrink, and, hence, fewer veterans will enroll in higher education.

Organization of Student Affairs.   We know from one of our studies (Kuh, Kinzie, Schuh, Whitt, & Associates, 2010) that student affairs can be organized in many ways and that new and innovative organizational structures have served institutions quite well (Manning, Kinzie, & Schuh, 2014). We think the days of student affairs being organized with a vice president who reports to the president may be in the past. That is not to say that a separate division of student affairs will not work on some campuses, because, quite obviously it will. Countless examples of this organizational structure exist and they meet their institution's administrative requirements and students' needs well. But we also think that a wider variety of organizational structures will be found in the future.

Institutional culture has a great effect on how student affairs is organized, as do an institution's mission and purpose (Manning et al., 2014). As institutions emphasize their distinctiveness (see Kalsbeek & Zucker, 2015), we think it is entirely likely that they will adopt new and innovative approaches to organization that could range from student-driven approaches to academic-driven models, particularly in the private, not-for-profit sector of higher education (Manning et al., 2014). Such institutional innovations call for new ways of thinking about student affairs work, how it is organized, who performs it—even how "student affairs work" is defined (Porterfield, Roper, & Whitt, 2011).

In addition, we do not categorically dismiss the value of student affairs units being included in the portfolio of the senior academic officer. Some might argue this form of organization does not appear to be in the best interests of student affairs units, but it can facilitate student and academic affairs collaboration, a critical organizational component to undergraduate student success (Kuh et al., 2010). We think this form of organization increasingly may be adapted where the president or chancellor wishes to foster greater collaboration between academic and student affairs on developing student learning experiences and/or wishes to have a designated senior officer of the institution focus on campus-based activities, potentially freeing another senior officer to focus on fundraising, legislative relations, or other external initiatives.

Financing Student Affairs.   The time period under consideration in this volume has hardly been a golden era for student affairs finance and we anticipate that institutions, regardless of their locus of control, will continue to find that developing a solid financial basis for student affairs is challenging. Student affairs has struggled over the years to compete on an even footing with academic and business affairs in the financial arena and we have no reason to believe that will change in the foreseeable future. Nevertheless, as Gansemer-Topf and Englin (Chapter 6) have pointed out, student affairs units make significant contributions to the learning and development of students; senior student affairs leaders must vigorously advocate for the critical role that their units play on their campuses.

We agree with Gansemer-Topf and Englin's observation that the strategy of automatically increasing fees may have hit its zenith. Shifting the costs of student affairs operations from tuition to student fees placated critics of the increasing costs of attendance for a period of time but as the total cost of attendance has undergone greater scrutiny in recent years, whether costs to students are part of tuition or mandatory fees is of little consequence to students and their parents. Practices such as automatically raising room and board rates to match inflation simply cannot be sustained in the current political environment. Gansemer-Topf and Englin have identified several strategies that student affairs educators may need to pursue more aggressively in the future, such as fundraising, to add to their revenue base. Their advice is well taken.

Programs. Making guesses about what the future might hold in terms of the programs and experiences in which students participate is a bit more daunting than examining enrollment and financial statistics and making predictions, primarily because data about programming are not collected with the regularity and pervasiveness of enrollment and financial data. Nevertheless, because of our involvement in several comprehensive studies (Kuh, Schuh, Whitt, & Associates, 1991; Kuh et al., 2010), we're prepared to take some guesses at what we think the future of programming might hold.

We think that because of its demonstrated potency, the learning community movement will continue to expand. Students who participate in learning communities are more likely to be retained and experience other desirable learning outcomes (Benjamin, 2015; Kuh, 2008). Therefore, we think learning communities represent splendid educational opportunities that result in benefits not only to students in terms of their learning but also to institutions in creating a highly desirable learning environment as measured by student retention from one year to the next.

We also believe that the future will see growth in experiential learning programs. Included in this set are such experiences as service learning programs, volunteer experiences, internships, and study abroad opportunities. All of these experiences have highly desirable learning outcomes such as self-efficacy, independence, and career development (see Pascarella & Terenzini, 2005, for a more complete discussion of outcomes related to these experiences). Perhaps equally important, employers of college graduates cite the importance—increasingly, the necessity—of practical experiences in which students apply in-class learning out of class for preparation for the world of work (Association of American Colleges and Universities [AAC&U], 2015).

It is difficult to predict the future of Greek letter organizations. Certainly these organizations have a place on many campuses and Cooperative Institutional Research Program results indicate that more than 13% of the participants indicated an interest in joining a fraternity or sorority (Eagan et al., 2014, p. 45). This percentage represents an increase of about 2% from the 2008 administration of the instrument (Pryor et al., 2008). Although these organizations are a fixture on many campuses, a seeming epidemic of high-profile incidents involving fraternity members—sexual assaults, racist behavior, vandalism, and so on—during the past 2 years has led to suspensions, even closures, of chapters on a number of campuses. A story published in *The Atlantic* in 2014, "The Dark Power of Fraternities," is just one example of the media attention being paid to these organizations (Flanagan, 2014). It's difficult to predict the long-term impact of increasing—and increasingly negative—media, public, and institutional focus on Greek life.

Technology. Cabellon and Junco (Chapter 5 in this volume) have highlighted interesting challenges for student affairs in the technology arena, particularly the use of "big data" in decision making and the capacity to develop increasingly nuanced understandings of students' experiences. We defer to their expertise on this topic, because the application of technology has become increasingly complex and difficult to understand for laypersons such as we are. In our time as the editorial leaders of this series, the use of technology has grown from the introduction of the Internet to electronic mail being the norm for communications (how often do you send or receive letters through the U.S. Postal Service?), to use of PowerPoint (and its descendants, such as Prezi) as the norm for presentations. Over that period of time, depiction of financial data via electronic spreadsheets and access to federal and other reports through the Internet have become routine. Websites, Facebook, and/or Twitter are the means by which many prospective students learn about colleges and universities. If you recall a college catalog and view book as the primary mechanisms by which students received information about prospective institutions, you are a member of our generation. The future belongs to digital technologies; as Junco (2014, p. 296) noted, "The best way for you as a student affairs professional to keep up with social technology development and adoption is to talk with your students."

Facilities. Many student affairs units are focused on the administration of facilities that provide services, programs, and learning opportunities for students. Among these units are student housing, campus unions, and campus recreation. Facilities have been built on many campuses that have resulted in substantial criticism of the costs and opulence associated with them (Finley, 2013). Vedder (2014, n.p.), in particular, has been critical of what he has characterized as the "country-clubization of the American university."

Given significant debt loads for many students (Institute for College Access & Success, 2014), we think it is likely that the days of lavish facilities are numbered. Facilities will be renovated, because many were built in the 1960s, but more restrained approaches to facility development will be employed. Revenues increasingly are tight and committing significant revenues to pay the debt service on sumptuous facilities may not prove to be a wise decision. We think facilities will be built or renovated with functionality and flexibility in mind, and we also think that such facilities will be constructed to support up-to-date technology, but we question the wisdom of over-the-top spending on dining and recreational facilities. We anticipate a more measured approach to facility development in the future.

Assessment. According to Peter Ewell (2009), and Becki Elkins in Chapter 4 of this sourcebook, the assessment movement in higher education began in the 1980s, although we can point to work of Aulepp and Delworth (1976) as an early marker in assessment in student affairs. Regardless, the commitment of student affairs staff and leaders to assessment gained momentum in the 1990s and in the first decade of this century and today is seen as an essential element of student affairs practice (Sandeen & Barr, 2006). We have no reason to believe that assessment will not be an essential element of student affairs practice beyond the foreseeable future.

Many reasons have been given for engaging in assessment in student affairs (see Upcraft & Schuh, 1996); Ewell (2009) has condensed the rationale for assessment in higher education to two critical issues: assessment for accountability and assessment for improvement. They effectively encapsulate all the many reasons given for assessment, including surviving; demonstrating cost effectiveness; measuring student needs; assessing student satisfaction; demonstrating the effectiveness of programs, policies, and practices; and so on (Upcraft & Schuh, 1996). We think Ewell's insight likely will carry the day as discussions about the need for assessment continue. We believe, too, that these two reasons for assessment are equally important. Student affairs units need to be able to satisfy their stakeholders that they are accomplishing what they set out to do, and they need to be committed to improvement as we found in our study of 20 high-performing institutions that were committed to continuously improving (Kuh et al., 2010).

We also believe that simply conducting studies and reporting findings without taking action will not suffice in the future. We share the concern expressed by Blaich and Wise (2011, p. 12): "The norm for many institutions is to gather data, to circulate the resulting reports among a small group of people, and then to just shelve them if nothing horrible jumps out—and sometimes even if it does!" In the future, student affairs staff and leaders will need to demonstrate not only that they are conducting assessments but also that they actually are making evidence-based changes that result in improved student learning. The more institution-specific programs are found to improve student learning, the more pervasive they will need to be, and that requires commitments and efforts by our institutions to our students.

Finally, we think assessments in student affairs in the future are likely to provide more information about student learning outcomes. Clearly, a focus on reporting student learning has been on the national agenda at least since the adoption of the report *A Test of Leadership* (U.S. Department of Education, 2006), and we believe that the future will see increased demand from various stakeholders who will seek more precise information from student affairs about what student learning results from participating in various programs, activities, and experiences. For example, what do students learn if they study abroad? What is the influence on students if they participate in service learning programs? What are the benefits from living in campus residence halls? We believe that the answers to these questions and others will be demanded by an increasingly savvy student body that will look at participation in the typical portfolio of experiences overseen by student affairs.

Conclusion

We ventured into making predictions with a great deal of trepidation because, despite our professional experiences, our reading of the literature, and our hunches, we have no real way of knowing if our predictions will be accurate or not! We are relatively certain that the pace of change in our institutions will continue to accelerate as has been the case during the combined 75 years we have served in administrative and faculty roles in higher education. We appreciate having had the opportunity to lead the *New Directions for Student Services* series since 1997, and as we turn the editorial roles over to Susan Jones and Sherry Watt, we thank our readers, our guest editors, our contributing authors, and, of course, the technical staff at Jossey-Bass for their continued support and interest in this series.

References

Association of American Colleges and Universities (AAC&U). (2015). *Falling short? College learning and career success.* Washington, DC: Author.

Aulepp, L., & Delworth, U. (1976). *Training manual for an ecosystem model.* Boulder, CO: WICHE.

Bell, D. (2013, January 30). "The wondrous world of 1990": A look at past predictions of the future. *U.S. News & World Report.* Retrieved from http://www.usnews.com/news/blogs/press-past/2013/01/30/the-wondrous-world-of-1990-a-look-at-past-predictions-of-the-future

Benjamin, M. (Ed.). (2015). *New Directions for Student Services: No. 148. Learning communities, start to finish.* San Francisco, CA: Jossey-Bass.

Blaich, C., & Wise, K. (2011). *From gathering to using assessment results: Lessons from the Wabash study.* Champaign, IL: University of Illinois and Indiana University, National Institute for Learning Outcomes Assessment.

Eagan, K., Stolzenberg, E. B., Ramirez, J. J., Aragon, M. C., Suchard, M. R., & Hurtado, S. (2014). *The American freshman: National norms fall 2014.* Los Angeles, CA: Higher Education Research Institute, UCLA.

Ewell, P. T. (2009). *Assessment, accountability improvement: Revisiting the tension.* Champaign, IL: University of Illinois and Indiana University, National Institute for Learning Outcomes Assessment.

Finley, A. (2013, August 28). Richard Vedder: The real reason college costs so much. *The Wall Street Journal*. Retrieved from http://www.wsj.com/articles/SB10001424127 8873246195045790292824385522674

Flanagan, C. (2014). The dark power of fraternities. *The Atlantic*. Retrieved from http://www.theatlantic.com/features/archive/2014/02/the-dark-power-of-fraternities /357580/

Hussar, W. J. (2002). *Pocket projections. Projections of education statistics to 2011* (NCES 2002–145). Washington, DC: U.S. Department of Education, National Center for Education Statistics.

Institute for College Access & Success. (2014). *The class of 2013*. Oakland, CA and Washington, DC: Author.

Jones, S. R., Harper, S. R., & Schuh, J. H. (2013). Shaping the future. In J. H. Schuh, S. R. Jones, & S. R. Harper (Eds.), *Student services: A handbook for the profession* (6th ed., pp. 534–546). San Francisco, CA: Jossey-Bass.

Junco, R. (2014). *Engaging students through social media*. San Francisco, CA: Jossey-Bass.

Kalsbeek, D. H., & Zucker, B. (2015). Markets and market niches. In D. Hossler & B. Bontrager (Eds.), *Handbook of strategic enrollment management* (pp. 77–102). San Francisco, CA: Jossey-Bass.

Kuh, G. D. (2008). *High-impact educational practices: What they are, who has access to them, and why they matter*. Washington, DC: Association of American Colleges and Universities.

Kuh, G. D., Kinzie, J., Schuh, J. H., Whitt, E. J., & Associates. (2010). *Student success in college: Creating conditions that matter*. San Francisco, CA: Jossey-Bass.

Kuh, G. D., Schuh, J. H., Whitt, E. J., & Associates. (1991). *Involving colleges: Successful approaches to fostering student learning and development outside the classroom*. San Francisco, CA: Jossey-Bass.

Manning, K., Kinzie, J., & Schuh, J. H. (2014). *One size does not fit all: Traditional and innovative models of student affairs practice* (2nd ed.). New York, NY: Routledge.

Myers, K. A., Lindburg, J. J., & Nied, D. M. (2013). *Allies for inclusion: Disability and equity in higher education* (ASHE Higher Education Report, Vol. 39, No. 5). San Francisco, CA: Jossey-Bass.

Pascarella, E. T., & Terenzini, P. T. (2005). *How college affects students* (Vol. 2). San Francisco, CA: Jossey-Bass.

Porterfield, K. T., Roper, L. D., & Whitt, E. J. (2011). Redefining our mission: What does higher education need from student affairs? *Journal of College and Character*, 12(4), 1–7.

Pryor, J. H., Hurtado, S., DeAngelo, L., Sharkness, J., Romero, L. C., Korn, W. K., & Tran, S. (2008). *The American freshman: National norms for fall 2008*. Los Angeles: University of California, Higher Education Research Institute.

Sandeen, A., & Barr, M. J. (2006). *Critical issues for student affairs*. San Francisco, CA: Jossey-Bass.

Silver, D. (2014, January 15). *College enrollment among low-income students still trails richer groups*. Pew Research Center FACTANK. Retrieved from http://www.pewresearch.org/fact-tank/2014/01/15/college-enrollment-among-low -income-students-still-trails-richer-groups

Snyder, T. D., & Dillow, S. A. (2013). *Digest of education statistics 2012* (NCES 2014-015). Washington, DC: National Center for Education Statistics, Institute of Education Sciences, U.S. Department of Education.

Snyder, T. D., Dillow, S. A., & Hoffman, C. M. (2009). *Digest of education statistics 2008* (NCES 2009-020). Washington, DC: U.S. Department of Education, Institute of Education Sciences, National Center for Education Statistics.

Task Force on the Future of Student Affairs. (2010). *Envisioning the future of student affairs*. Washington, DC: ACPA and NASPA.

Upcraft, M. L., & Schuh, J. H. (1996). *Assessment in student affairs*. San Francisco, CA: Jossey-Bass.

U.S. Department of Education. (2006). *A test of leadership*. Washington, DC: U.S. Department of Education, Secretary's Commission on the Future of Higher Education.

Vedder, R. (2014). *The coming crisis in American higher education*. Remarks made to the Ohio Association of Scholars, Columbus, OH. Retrieved January 6, 2015, from http://centerforcollegeaffordability.org/2014/10/22/12755/

ELIZABETH J. WHITT *is vice provost and dean for undergraduate education and professor of sociology at the University of California, Merced.*

JOHN H. SCHUH *is director of the Emerging Leaders Academy and distinguished professor emeritus at Iowa State University.*

NEW DIRECTIONS FOR STUDENT SERVICES • DOI: 10.1002/ss

INDEX

Strauss, J., 72
Strauss, W., 29
Stringer, J., 49, 50, 58
Strohl, J., 36
Student Affairs and Higher Education Administration (SA-HE), 84
Student affairs assessment: current state of, 42–44; future perspective, 44–46; history of, 39–42; overview, 39; predictions for, 96–97; stages of, 42–43; student learning outcomes, evidence of, 43–44
Student Affairs Assessment Leaders (SAAL), 41
Student affairs educators, preparation of: accreditation and professional competencies, 83–84; curricula, changes in, 81–82; doctoral preparation, 84–85; experiential options, 82–83; graduate preparation, future of, 86–87; graduate program enrollments, 80–81; master's-level preparation, changes in, 80–84; overview, 79–80; professional development, trends in, 85–86
Student affairs practice: accountability, 20–21; assessment in, 20–22; change in, 91–97; facilities, predictions for, 95–96; future of, 89–97; global engagements and sustainability, 22–23; higher education cost and access, 15–17; organization of, 93; overview, 15; programs, predictions for, 94–95; recommendations for, 23–24; student learning and development, 17–18; unbounded learning environments, promotion of, 18–20
Student characteristics: assessment of student experiences, 30–31; conceptions of, over time, 27–31; demographic trends, 28–29; emphasis on, of NDSS, 31–33; generational perspective, 29–30; implications of, 35–36; overview, 27; predictions for, 91–93; sociohistorical context, 29; student

affairs, responses of, 33–35; student attitudes and values, 30; student development research and student needs, 31
Student Services, 91
Student Success in College: Creating Conditions That Matter, 75
Suchard, M. R., 95
Suskie, L., 40

Tagg, J., 40
Take Back Higher Education, 18
Tatro vs. University of Minnesota, 54
Terenzini, P. T., 19, 20, 94
Test of Leadership, A, 97
Thomas, A. G., 55
Tinker vs. Des Moines Independent County School District, 54
Tinto, V., 52
Titus, M. A., 70
Tran, S., 95
Tschepikow, W. K., 40
Tull, A., 50, 55, 86
Twenge, J., 29

Upcraft, M. L., 39, 40, 45, 96

Vedder, R., 95
Vesper, N., 19

Walker, D. A., 84
Wesaw, A. J., 84, 86, 87
Whalen, E., 72
Whitt, E. J., 2, 3, 14, 19, 21, 22, 45, 75, 89, 93, 94, 96, 99
Wise, K., 96
Wishon, G. D., 58
Wright, B. D., 40, 45

Zapata, L. P., 55
Zerulik, J. D., 41
Ziskin, M., 15
Zucker, B., 93

SS150 **Understanding and Addressing Commuter Student Needs**
J. Patrick Biddix
Despite representing a majority of the college student population, a surprising lack of research has focused on the unique issues and needs of commuter students. This volume reviews the contemporary research and thinking about commuter students. The topics include:
• theoretical perspectives and discussions of foremost topics and issues,
• specific examples for applying contemporary research with students of color, students with disabilities, and online students,
• perspectives for immediate work and strategic planning, and
• practical applications, recommendations, and suggestions for supporting commuter students.
The volume has four major sections: theory, profiles and issues, support and services, and general applications. While the volume updates and adds to the collective scholarship on commuter students, the primary purpose is to offer guidance for practitioners and scholars.
ISBN 978-11191-15199

SS149 **Learning Communities from Start to Finish**
Mimi Benjami
The pairing of the words "learning" and "community" speaks volumes about what we value and are trying to achieve through higher education. "Learning" is the primary mission of our institutions, and while the platforms for learning continue to evolve, we recognize that learning typically is not a solitary process. The element of "community" in our educational endeavors provides support, information, and opportunities to practice skills that are both academic and personal. While the phrase "learning communities" has various definitions, at the heart of all programs is the goal of enhancing the student learning experience in the community of others.
  This volume provides valuable information about learning communities "from start to finish," including:
• historical and theoretical foundations that guide these programs,
• structures of learning communities that provide varied opportunities for student participation, with a focus on specific student populations who may benefit from learning community experiences, and
• elements of staffing and assessment, as well as an annotated bibliography of recent learning community literature.
The authors consider critical elements of learning community programs and offer recommendations and options for faculty and staff who work with, or hope to work with, this particular curricular and cocurricular learning structure.
ISBN 978-11190-65111

ORDER FORM SUBSCRIPTION AND SINGLE ISSUES

DISCOUNTED BACK ISSUES:

Use this form to receive 20% off all back issues of *New Directions for Student Services*.
All single issues priced at **$23.20** (normally $29.00)

TITLE	ISSUE NO.	ISBN

Call 1-800-835-6770 or see mailing instructions below. When calling, mention the promotional code JBNND to receive your discount. For a complete list of issues, please visit www.josseybass.com/go/ndss

SUBSCRIPTIONS: (1 YEAR, 4 ISSUES)

☐ New Order ☐ Renewal

U.S.	☐ Individual: $89	☐ Institutional: $335
CANADA/MEXICO	☐ Individual: $89	☐ Institutional: $375
ALL OTHERS	☐ Individual: $113	☐ Institutional: $409

Call 1-800-835-6770 or see mailing and pricing instructions below.
Online subscriptions are available at www.onlinelibrary.wiley.com

ORDER TOTALS:

Issue / Subscription Amount: $ _____

Shipping Amount: $ _____
(for single issues only – subscription prices include shipping)

Total Amount: $ _____

SHIPPING CHARGES:	
First Item	$6.00
Each Add'l Item	$2.00

(No sales tax for U.S. subscriptions. Canadian residents, add GST for subscription orders. Individual rate subscriptions must be paid by personal check or credit card. Individual rate subscriptions may not be resold as library copies.)

BILLING & SHIPPING INFORMATION:

☐ **PAYMENT ENCLOSED:** *(U.S. check or money order only. All payments must be in U.S. dollars.)*

☐ **CREDIT CARD:** ☐ VISA ☐ MC ☐ AMEX

Card number _____Exp. Date_____

Card Holder Name_____Card Issue # _____

Signature _____Day Phone_____

☐ **BILL ME:** *(U.S. institutional orders only. Purchase order required.)*

Purchase order # _____
      Federal Tax ID 13559302 • GST 89102-8052

Name_____

Address_____

Phone_____ E-mail_____

Copy or detach page and send to: **John Wiley & Sons, One Montgomery Street, Suite 1000, San Francisco, CA 94104-4594**

Order Form can also be faxed to: **888-481-2665**

PROMO JBNND

Great Resources for Higher Education Professionals

dent Affairs Today

sues for $225 (print) / $180 (e)

nnovative best practices
udent affairs plus lawsuit
maries to keep your institution
f legal trouble. It's packed
advice on offering effective
ces, assessing and funding
ams, and meeting legal
rements.

ntaffairstodaynewsletter.com

Campus Legal Advisor

12 issues for $210 (print) / $170 (e)

From complying with the ADA
and keeping residence halls
safe to protecting the privacy of
student information, this monthly
publication delivers proven
strategies to address the tough
legal issues you face on campus.

campuslegaladvisor.com

Campus Security Report

12 issues for $210 (print) / $170 (e)

A publication that helps you
effectively manage the challenges
in keeping your campus, students,
and employees safe. From
protecting students on campus
after dark to interpreting the latest
laws and regulations, *Campus
Security Report* has answers
you need.

campussecurityreport.com

ional Teaching & Learning Forum

ues for $65 (print or e)

big concepts to practical details and from
ng-edge techniques to established wisdom,
is your resource for cross-disciplinary discourse
udent learning. With it, you'll gain insights into
ing theory, classroom management, lesson
ing, scholarly publishing, team teaching,
e learning, pedagogical innovation, technology,
nore.

om

Disability Compliance for Higher Education

12 issues for $230 (print) / $185 (e)

This publication combines interpretation of disability
laws with practical implementation strategies to help
you accommodate students and staff with disabilities.
It offers data collection strategies, intervention models
for difficult students, service review techniques,
and more.

disabilitycomplianceforhighereducation.com

n & Provost

sues for $225 (print) / $180 (e)

budgeting to faculty tenure and from distance
ing to labor relations, *Dean & Provost* gives
nnovative ways to manage the challenges of
ng your institution. Learn how to best use limited
rces, safeguard your institution from frivolous
uits, and more.

ndprovost.com

Enrollment Management Report

12 issues for $230 (print) / $185 (e)

Find out which enrollment strategies are working
for your colleagues, which aren't, and why. This
publication gives you practical guidance on all
aspects—including records, registration, recruitment,
orientation, admissions, retention, and more.

enrollmentmanagementreport.com

WANT TO SUBSCRIBE?
Go online or call: 888.378.2537.

JB JOSSEY-BASS™
A Wiley Brand

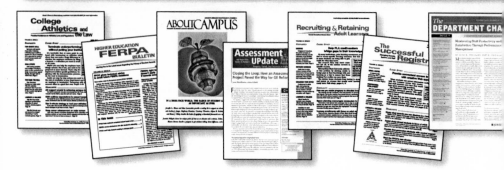